"Verne Harnish's lessons helped me grow iGo Revenues 100% a year for seven years while having fun and building a great team. Any entrepreneur who wants to accelerate their business should check out Verne's teachings and Masters of Business Dynamics Program. I learned the analytics and theories of business at Stanford Business School, I learned how to apply them in a real world fast growth company with Verne's Masters of Business Dynamics program."

KEN HAWK, FOUNDER, JUNIPER VENTURES
RENO, NEVADA

"Verne Harnish is a clear thinker. He helped me understand the 'habits' that enabled me to build my business."

JEFFREY DENNIS, PRESIDENT, FLAGSHIP CAPITAL PARTNERS INC.
TORONTO, ONTARIO, CANADA

"The tools you have given Event Network have become cornerstones of our growth and ingrained in our culture."

LARRY GILBERT, PRESIDENT & CEO, EVENT NETWORK
LA JOLLA, CALIFORNIA

"Verne teaches basic principles, honesty in all your endeavors, and a human touch that has helped the company stay on course."

FRANSISCO ESTEBAN LAINEZ, LABORATORIOS Y DROGUERIA LAINEZ, S.A. DE C.V.
EL SALVADOR

"The daily meetings, weekly meetings and quarterly/retreat meetings with the executives and then cascading the same meeting structure to the subsequent levels of management and employees have given Pilgrim Software, Inc. the discipline needed to communicate the company's direction, tackle day-to-day operation issues and promote a sense of urgency effectively. Everybody who is involved provides positive feedback on this new change."

AMI UTJI, CEO & PRESIDENT, PILGRIM SOFTWARE, INC.
TAMPA, FLORIDA

"Verne's entrepreneurial insights have helped businesses all over the globe grow to the next level. This is a book you will want to read and study."

TODD HOPKINS, FOUNDER & CEO, OFFICE PRIDE COMMERCIAL CLEANING SERVICES
FRANKLIN, INDIANA

"I have been applying the 'Mastering a One-Page Strategic Plan,' and every time I repeat our core values it seems to over motivate our employees and customers, the benefits are immediate."

JORGE R. ARRIAZA
CORPORACION LOS PROCERES, S. A.

"Verne has a unique gift to turn complex problems into simple solutions. I have always walked away from his sessions with a much clearer idea of what I needed to do as a CEO."

SAM GOODNER, PRESIDENT & CEO, CATAPULT SYSTEMS
AUSTIN, TEXAS

"Verne told me things that I have never heard before. His simplistic yet revolutionary approach to the fundamentals of business is head spinning! After really digesting what Verne taught me, I immediately strategically positioned my company for what I now know ultimately will happen on the course of rapid growth."

BRUCE SMITH, PRESIDENT AND CEO, SAFETY VISION, LP
HOUSTON, TEXAS

"I have introduced a number of tools that Verne has provided to our management staff. This has allowed us to create the foundation which is critical in building a successful company."

SCOTT S. SMITH, PRESIDENT, COALITION AMERICA, INC.
ATLANTA, GEORGIA

"The entrepreneurial experience can be exciting and rewarding while at the same time lonely and tragic. Through Verne Harnish's leadership programs the opportunity to come together with like-minded business leaders and harness our collective energy within proven frameworks is second to none."

BRIAN J. HANSELL, EXECUTIVE VICE-PRESIDENT, BALL HARRISON HANSELL
BURLINGTON, ONTARIO, CANADA

"The knowledge I gained from Verne's materials has provided me with fantastic insight both for my business and my personal well-being. I take full advantage of any opportunity I have to learn from Verne."

BRAD SCHY, THE TICKET MAESTRO, MUSICAL CHAIRS TICKET SERVICE
BRENTWOOD, CALIFORNIA

"Start to Scale helped put focus and spark back into my firm—a must for languishing entrepreneurs!"

MARIE MINICHINO, CEO, BELLAMARIAINT.COM
MAUI, HAWAII

"A must-read for every entrepreneur that wants to create a successful company."

DANIEL A. MARCOS, COUNTRY MANAGER,
MEXICO PATAGON

"Verne's Tools have made a dramatic and effective difference in my company. They have aligned everyone from the top to the bottom and focused us on our daily behaviors, which precede our most audacious goals."

WILL ANDREW, PRESIDENT, WAC SPORTWEAR
TORONTO, ONTARIO, CANADA

"You have a true sense of the needs of growing businesses, and your presented topics are exactly on the mark. Upon learning your tactics, we immediately implemented changes to our systems and achieved very positive results."

RICK RESTELLI, INTERNATIONAL APPAREL COMPANY
PITTSBURGH, PENNSYLVANIA

"I was able to return to my company with a renewed enthusiasm and apply a proven methodology to help move my organization to the next level. By applying the principles, we were able to have a concentrated focus on an area that we needed to improve to stay ahead of our competitors. The principles have proven logical and I got the results I was looking for."

MICHELE NICKLIS, PRESIDENT & CEO, TRI-QSI
CARY, NORTH CAROLINA

"If you measure success in terms of 'take home value,' Verne's work is A+. Fiberlink would not be the company we are without Verne. He helped us understand the challenges and changing dynamics as the company grew from 10 to 50 to 125 employees. His predictions and prescriptions were spot on and proved the ultimate in preventive medicine."

JIM SHEWARD, CEO, FIBERLINK BLUE BELL,
PENNSYLVANIA

"Our daily huddles have created an organization that takes the same breath every day. We no longer have to "figure out" who is doing what & when... we know."

LORNE ZALESIN, VICE PRESIDENT, BILTMORE PROPERTIES CORPORATION
TROY, MICHIGAN

"After my first session with Verne, we immediately made several fundamental changes to our organization and the definition of its objectives. Without that kind of correction, we would surely have struggled much harder through the fast growth phase of our business."

DAVE GHEESLING, PRESIDENT & CEO, FLOOREXPO, INC.
LITHIA SPRINGS, GEORGIA

"Verne's concepts can be applied to any company at any time for near immediate results."

KEITH RINZLER, MEDIAVEHICLES.COM
ATLANTA, GEORGIA

"Verne's specific business tools and commandments were so concrete that putting them into effect in our office had an immediate measurable impact on the business and our people. With Verne's help we set a goal of expanding, profitably, to six cities in one year. Our executive staff is now working together to keep each other, and our business on track for the next goals in our long-term vision of a mature business."

PETE PATTERSON, PRESIDENT & CEO, CAPITAL RECOVERY GROUP
HOUSTON, TEXAS

"Verne sketched his quarterly planning outline for me on the back of a napkin, and two weeks later all of my employees were applauding my new master plan. All of Verne's tools are simple and brilliant, and Verne is simply brilliant."

RAYMOND KING, FOUNDER AND PAST CEO OF SEMAPHORE, INC.,
CO-FOUNDER OF SNAPNAMES.COM, INC.
PORTLAND, OREGON

"From strategic goal alignment to our daily communication plan, Verne's practical ideas were key in building our two-time Inc. 500 company."

TOM SALONEK, CEO, GO-E-BIZ.COM
ST. PAUL, MINNESOTA

"Business management is a vastly complex undertaking. Harnish's tools, methodologies and simple truisms (like 'Doing the Right Things Right') help eliminate what can be the blinding complexities, and in turn bring clarity to the process of aligning, and better managing the business enterprise."

MARK D. GORDON, CHIEF ENERGIZING OFFICER, SYNERGY NETWORKS, INC.
VIENNA, VIRGINIA

"Verne's tools helped me more than any other business educational tool I have ever used. In just a few short days of exposure to his teaching, I was able to go home and begin a revolution that would prove to change our company for the better for the balance of time."

BILL HUDSON JR., CEO, HUDSON SALVAGE INC.
HATTIESBURG, MISSISSIPPI

"Verne Harnish supplies the mental tools to grow and prosper—I am living proof."

RUSSELL VAIL, PRESIDENT, CLEARSAIL COMMUNICATIONS, LLC
HOUSTON, TEXAS

"This is very powerful stuff! If you don't believe me, ask any one on my management team."

ROB SOLOMON, CHAIRMAN, USOL HOLDINGS, INC.
AUSTIN, TEXAS

"To grow and lead a successful business, I recognize the need for professional and business development activities. I have met many business consultants and regularly attend many leadership programs. Verne's advice and guidance, stands out from the pack. In this book Verne provides the most potent, practical insight and direction necessary for growing a business with focus, accountability and rhythm."

RICHARD M. BRUEGGMAN, DATA SCIENCE AUTOMATION, INC.
CANONSBURG, PENNSYLVANIA

"With this material we redefined our market niche through a uniquely sustainable competitive advantage and grew our revenue over 50% in the first year of implementation."

JEFF STEPLER, PRESIDENT, TELCOM TRAINING CORPORATION
IRVING, TEXAS

"Working with companies like AOL, NBC, Gateway, sophisticated investors and others, it has become clear to me that execution is the most critical strategic weapon. Verne has been instrumental in mastering and transferring the visionary and executionary tools and habits that have allowed my companies to succeed where others have failed. A database is nothing without an effective execution plan."

GREGORY CARSON, CEO, CITL, INC.
NEW YORK, NEW YORK

"We have begun to make many of the changes that I learned from Verne. We did the whole planning pyramid and 45 days later the 400 plus employees can now recite what the key measures are and what our brand promise is. Even more impressive is that people are behaving differently. It is so simple it is beautiful!"

JOHN STEPLETON, PRESIDENT, RESEARCH DATA DESIGN, INC.

"Many companies suffer from their inability to benchmark. Verne's business fundamentals helped us to learn to benchmark while understanding where to buy the lumber and make it square. We've been sitting pretty ever since!"

MAURICE GLAVIN, TOTAL SCOPE, INC.
BOORWYN, PENNSYLVANIA

"Verne's work allowed us to focus and articulate our vision and plans for the company. We struggled for months to get our hands around the project. Verne's tools assisted us in pulling together the strategic plan of TimeVision in a concise, understandable format. Now we can spend the time executing and not struggling with definitions."

LOIS MELBOURNE, PRESIDENT & CEO, TIMEVISION, INC.
IRVING, TEXAS

"As a CEO of a fast growth company (four year rate 871%), finding the one "choke point" has allowed us to focus the whole company on maximizing our competitive advantage. Thanks to Verne, we should be growing at four digits in the coming year."

SAMUEL CHANG, CEO, WISDOM CLOTHING COMPANY
DULLES, VIRGINIA

"Verne is an outstanding student of business, and his abundant findings frequently translate into business initiatives for our company."

TIM HANDLEY, CHAIRMAN & CEO, ADVANTAGE COMPANIES

"When growing a profitable company seems its most demanding and complex, Verne is a master of providing simple tools to make it all seem possible and a lot easier to accomplish."

JEFF FREEMYER, CEO, CONVERGENT MEDIA SYSTEMS
ATLANTA, GEORGIA

"Verne's enterprise building tools helped create controls that identified large holes in our systems and procedures. Once identified, we saved millions annually and the savings continue to multiply today."

HAROLD SOLOMON, SERAPHIM PARTNERS, LLC
ATLANTA, GEORGIA

"Verne Harnish's toolbox for businesses provided our company the keys to building a solid team in a fast growth environment, which enabled us to jump to the front of the line in our market-place. His leadership has inspired entrepreneurs through out the world and the results have been immeasurable!"

MICHAEL J. MALONE, CHAIRMAN & CEO, MJM INVESTIGATIONS, INC.
MORRISVILE, NORTH CAROLINA

"Verne Harnish is without a doubt the clearest thinker in entrepreneurial education and develop-ment today."

SCOTT TANNAS, CADVISION
CALGARY, ALBERTA, CANADA

"Our daily five-minute huddles have been going on now for two years. The huddle provides the opportunity to report critical numbers that affect the overall goals and objectives of our compa-ny while fostering rhythm, alignment and team building of our employees. Before implementing our five-minute huddles our monthly meetings would last over five hours, now it's down to 90 minutes."

MICHAEL CABRERA, PRESIDENT & CEO, ANCICARE PPO, INC.
MIRAMAR, FLORIDA

"Verne fostered an environment that encouraged entrepreneurism with discipline, which has been highly effective for my company."

DEVIN SCHAIN, CEO, ON CAMPUS MARKETING
BETHESDA, MARYLAND

"Learning from Verne how to Master the Rockefeller Habits propelled my company farther ahead in one week than we had moved the entire past year. We never used to have scheduled meetings. Using the Rockefeller Habits to establish a meeting rhythm really aligned our management team. Now we can't live without our daily huddle and weekly 'Hour of Power.'"

ROGER SCHEUMANN, PRESIDENT & OWNER, QUARTERMAINE COFFEE ROASTERS
ROCKVILLE, MARYLAND

"These tools helped me set goals for the organization and then meet them, for example, make the Inc. 500, raise capital to scale the company, and once funded, open multiple centers to be better poised for acquisition."

JEANNE LAMBERT, PRESIDENT & CEO, CERIDA CORPORATION
ANDOVER, MASSACHUSETTS

"Verne is the master of 'actionable' tools. His practical advice has helped align our firm around what's important and energized our team to reach for what they thought was impossible. Verne himself is a gazelle among gazelles."

JOHN WARRILLOW, PRESIDENT, WARRILLOW & CO., INC.
TORONTO, ONTARIO, CANADA

"Verne is able to put into words some of things that are hard to express but you know are just good common sense when it comes to business. His presentations and tools have helped me commu-nicate these ideas more effectively throughout my organization."

JOHN SCIARABBA, ALDEN SYSTEMS

"Verne's tools and material transformed not only our company but also all our clients."

EROS KAW, MANAGING PARTNER, ROXAS AND KAW
PHILIPPINES

"Sometimes the simplest ideas are the best ideas. In a short period of time I have implemented the Rockefeller Habits into our corporate structure and into my personal planning. I find myself more focused on the most important task, and communication has increased within our organization."

GARY GREGG, PRESIDENT, APPLEONE EMPLOYMENT SERVICES
TORONTO, ONTARIO, CANADA

"Not only do the tools help realign the firm, they also help realign the way you think about business and life."

JIM BAKER, PRESIDENT, ASG, INC.
CARY, NORTH CAROLINA

"The laser focus gleaned from Verne's master habits is propelling and aligning my company to reach higher levels more quickly than I had ever imagined possible."

BOB THORDARSON, CEO, CONSUMERWARE
KIRKLAND, WASHINGTON

"The Rockefeller Habits are concise tools for my management toolbox. The communication tools improved our behavior, and performance, forever! Understanding myself better, has helped me to understand and interact with others at an entirely different level."

ANDREW MARTIN, PRESIDENT & CEO, ATM GROUP, INC.

"Fifteen minutes with Verne Harnish is more valuable than attending fifteen years of business school. His teachings and theories are straightforward, completely relevant, easy to apply, eye opening and somewhat terrifying. I am sure this book will not disappoint and prove invaluable to the business owner who reads it."

CHRISTINE DIMMICK, PRESIDENT, THE GOOD HOME CO., INC.
NEW YORK, NEW YORK

"Adopting the mastering series has been an amazing venture. Our organization has become a laser-focused machine. The energy is electric! "

SUZANNE M. LAUBERTH, FISTER LAUBERTH, INC.
ST. LOUIS, MISSOURI

"Without implementing Verne's 15-minute daily conference call at the same time every day for our nine key managers at three different locations, we could not have grown our operation as smoothly or as quickly as we have. We have over 600 employees that depend on a unified management team."

DAVID GARFINKLE MITCHEL, LINCOLN PACKAGING LTD.
MONTREAL, QUÉBEC, CANADA

"My company immediately put Verne's Rockefeller Habits into action. We made more money and got more accomplished, but that is nothing compared to the level of satisfaction and fun that my entire team immediately benefited from."

GREGORY C. MORAN, PRESIDENT, PCS GROUP INC., PINNACLE TECHNOLOGY SOLUTIONS
TROY, NEW YORK

"Verne reveals the dos and don'ts of growing a business. We know better what to do as we grow, because of the lessons learned from others' mistakes and successes."

JOEL STEVENS, PC OUTLET INC. AND PC OUTLET LLC
RICHMOND HILL, ONTARIO, CANADA

"I was amazed by what kinds of effects a few simple ideas, consistently applied, can have on my company. We are now much more focused, our goals and objectives are clearer, and you might even argue that our management team and staff efforts are aligned!"

JEFF BEHRENS, PRESIDENT, THE TELLURIDE GROUP, INC.
NEWTON, MASSACHUSETTS

"We are on course for an 86% increase in net profit, thanks to Verne Harnish's training."

THOMAS P. RIETZ, PRESIDENT & CEO, CANTERRA HOMES, INC.
SCOTTSDALE, ARIZONA

"Verne Harnish has made a huge difference in our company by shaping our strategic direction. He helped our leadership see the big picture of the business environment and greatly expand our horizon."

PETER PHILLIPS, PRESIDENT, THE PHILLIPS GROUP
MIDDLETOWN, PENNSYLVANIA

"Verne Harnish is a visionary. His work inspired me to listen to my inner wisdom and helped me to develop the habits and skills to support success in every area of my life."

MARLA DURDEN, PROFOUND HARVEST, INC.
SEATTLE, WASHINGTON

"Within one week of implementing these tools I felt dramatic effects! It was quite amazing how everything crystallized within a few months. Our clients even began to comment on the success of our consultants and the new level of servicing we were able to offer. I have told many others about these wonderful tools who have since implemented them and found staggering results. It is almost impossible to imagine running a business without them."

KRISTINE DOYLE, MAVEN, INC.
NEW YORK, NEW YORK

"Verne is simply one of the best at getting companies aligned. Everything he does has unparalleled energy and substance to it—a necessity when you are trying to build a successful business. We were a nice little well run company (or so we thought) until I met Verne Harnish, and then the bomb dropped (let's just say we had limitless opportunities for improvement). The good news is after implementing Verne's techniques, we have become a very efficiently run business, and are poised to make some big waves in our industry."

RANDY NELSON, ORION INTERNATIONAL
RALEIGH, NORTH CAROLINA

"With all the challenges of driving a rapidly growing global business, the alignment we have created between our international offices by utilizing the Rockefeller Habits has been hugely successful."

BRYAN HANSEL, CEO, V I R D E V
EAGAN, MINNESOTA

START
TO
SCALE

Secrets to Starting and Scaling Any Size Organization

Verne Harnish

Forbes | Books

Start to Scale
Copyright 2024 © by Verne Harnish

This edition published by Forbes Books
An imprint of Advantage Media Group.

Forbes Books is a registered trademark, and the Forbes Books
colophon is a trademark of Forbes Media, LLC.

Third Edition

ISBN 979-8-88750-676-0 (Paperback)
ISBN: 979-8-88750-677-7 (eBook)

Library of Congress Control Number: 2024918159

Library of Congress Cataloging-in-Publication Data
Harnish, Verne
Start to Scale

Manufactured in the United States of America 20 19 18

ACKNOWLEDGEMENTS

To my children, Cameron, Cole, Jade and Quinn,
who continue to help me rediscover fundamentals.

A lifetime surrounded by business owners has shaped the thoughts in this book, starting with both my grandparents who each had their own small businesses and my father, a partner in a successful firm for years that collapsed within months when a major customer's funds were frozen by a government agency, leaving dad's firm without the "oxygen" it needed to continue its rapid growth.

Along the way, key business mentors continued to share their wisdom, including Bill Woods, Don Simpson, Willard Garvey, and Fran Jabara, the founder of the Center for Entrepreneurship at Wichita State University. It was through my association with Fran that I was exposed to the business savvy of George Ablah, Dan Carney, Frank Carney, Jack DeBoer, Tom Devlin, Larry Jones, Charles Koch, and other highly visible and successful Wichita entrepreneurs and business leaders.

Since then, I must acknowledge the thousands of entrepreneurs that have participated in the Association of Collegiate Entrepreneurs (ACE), Entrepreneurs Organization (EO), and the Entrepreneurial Masters' Program (EMP) held at MIT. I'll always remember those early annual and highly instructive presentations by Michael Dell and the moving presentation by Steve Jobs, as he described the creation of Apple and his subsequent firing, in front of over 1100 students and young entrepreneurs from around the world. Key business mentors during this time included Arthur Lipper and Bernie Goldhirsh, founders of two of the most important publications of the entrepreneurship movement, and Dr. Warren Winstead and Dr. Rudy Lamone who guided the building of the Entrepreneurs Organization and supported my teaching at the University of Maryland.

Special acknowledgement must go to those that have invested in our work at Gazelles (now Scaling Up) including Nick Alexos, Jamie Coulter, Ted Leonsis, John Street, and Alan Trefler and to our early board of advisors including Boyd Clarke, John Cone, Tom Delaney, Dan Garner, Howard Getson, Gene Kirila, Andrew Sherman, and Bob Verdun. In addition, several business thought leaders have contributed their thinking and have been ongoing faculty members for the MIT program and/or Master of Business Dynamics (MBD) program including Dr. Ed Roberts, Dr. Vince Fulmer, Dr. John van Maanen, Dr. Bill Isaacs, Dr. Barbara Bund, Dr. Barrie Greiff, Dr. Neil Churchill, Jack Stack, Don Peppers, Martha Rogers, Jim Kouzes, George Naddaff, Gary Hirshberg, Aubrey Daniels, Randy Fields, Jimmy Calano, Geoff Smart, Duane Boyce, Jack Little, Stuart Moore, and Pat Lencioni. And I've always gained practical business insights from the work of Steve Mariotti and his Network for Teaching Entrepreneurship (NFTE). This book would not have been possible without the help and support of the original Gazelles team which included Nicole Pascale, Rob Main, and Blanca Dec. Thanks also to Cindy Anderson who loaned a copy of and encouraged me to read Titan, the biography of John D. Rockefeller. And there is always an important and patient team that makes the actual book possible including Ellen Wojahn, who helped with the writing of the Mightywords articles that led to this book. Many thanks to the current team at Forbes Books including Adam Witty, Evan Schnittman, Beth LaGuardia, and Elisabeth Lynch. Jun-Hi Lutterjohann for the revised cover design and layout; Elaine Pofeldt for supporting in writing and editing; and Jean Santos for proofreading.

CONTENTS

INTRODUCTION

A PRACTICAL PERFORMANCE PLATFORM

After burning out on two consecutive businesses, Dave Rogenmoser and his two partners, JP Morgan and Chris Hull, decided to start over again.

They launched another business but quickly experienced too much hassle and stress again. This time, however, they turned to the Scaling Up approach for answers. The result? In a 36-hour session, they created a business that proved scalable and fun to run.

"I think at the end of 2016, exhausted again, we just kind of said: if we keep going like this, we don't really want to do this anymore. This is too much work and too much hassle and stress. And so we said: well, let's just try this Scaling Up approach for three months and just see how it goes."

The biggest gains according to Dave (with the eventual help of a coach), is more clarity, improved communication, better alignment, more freedom, and less stress.

"I think without this methodology, we probably would have left that three-day retreat not really having any clear outcome. But even if we did, I don't think we would've had the structure to go make it happen."

Speed forward five years and a pivot to AI driven content, Dave raised $125 million at a $1.5 billion valuation to continue scaling Jasper.

From Startup to Scaleup to Unicorn—Easier with Less Drama

Dave's story is one of 102,000+ firms, of all sizes, industries, and geographies, that have used the Scaling Up to successfully scale easier with less drama.

Our Performance Platform provides a 100% solution for organizations, whether just starting out or scaling to billion-dollar valuations. And it's a platform that scales with you—so you're not having to switch language or routines to maintain momentum.

Leaders and employees of growing firms want ideas and tools they can implement immediately to improve some aspect of their business. Less theory; more how-to.

Tools that Effect Change

The term "tools" is a deliberate label and comes from a favorite Buckminster Fuller quote that embodies our change management philosophy, "If you want to teach people a new way of thinking, don't bother trying to teach them. Instead, give them a tool, the use of which will lead to new ways of thinking." The tools you are about to learn will affect real and positive changes in your business.

Real and Immediate Results—Why Believe?

Yet why believe these tools are useful? At the front of this book are over one-hundred CEO endorsements for the tools you'll be acquiring in this book – and many more case studies/articles posted on *www.scaleups.com*. These are just some of the over 820,000 leaders who have put our tools to work. We know how important authentic references are to the leaders of start-up to mid-size firms. You need to know that what you're going to spend your time learning and implementing actually works in real companies like yours.

Short and Sweet

Like this introduction, I'll not waste a lot of words. The material is structured so you can scan it quickly, pick-up the ideas that matter, and have one-page tools you can use to implement those ideas. Except for Chapter 1, which provides an example-rich overview of the application of our tools, the rest of the chapters are structured into bite-sized chunks of information with a liberal use of subheadings and summaries. Enjoy your exploration of these tools.

Weekly Insights

If you like the style and substance of the book, you can receive a very concise weekly email of best practices for leading a growing firm—ideas I pick up each week from leaders like you. To receive, please send an email to: *verne@ScalingUp.com* and put "Weekly Insights" in the subject line. And please include a first and last name, your title and tell us where your company is based. We'll add you to our expanding list of leaders of scaling companies.

OVERVIEW

SUMMARY OF KEY TAKEAWAYS

(Reading this chapter provides a summary for those who want to just scan the rest of the book)

What is the underlying handful of fundamentals that drive everything else that's important in business? What is still fundamental today in scaling a successful firm that hasn't changed for over a hundred years? Let me triangulate my answer while providing an overview of the book's key concepts.

Tom Meredith, former CFO of Dell Computer, and I were discussing how the fundamentals in creating a great business are the same for parenting great kids. Early in his career before Dell, his wife had encouraged him to attend a Parent Effectiveness Training (PET) program. Reluctantly, he attended. However, what he discovered were some fundamentals that were just as applicable in business as at home—so much so that he purchased copies for all the executives where he worked.

Anyone with children will recognize the fundamentals I've summarized as:

1. Have a handful of rules
2. Repeat yourself a lot
3. Act consistently with those rules
   (which is why you better have only a few rules)

Two decades later Walter Isaacson, who wrote the must-read biography on Steve Jobs, penned an equally important biography on

Elon Musk. Both modern titans of business exhibited a set of disciplines underlying what we've seen are key to scaling any organization:

Priorities—Does the organization have objective Top 3-5 priorities for the year and the quarter (the month if growing over 100% annually) and a clear Top 1 priority along with an appropriate Theme? Does everyone in the organization have their own handful of priorities that align with the company's priorities?

Data—Does the organization have sufficient data on a daily and weekly basis to provide insight into how the organization is running and what the market is demanding? Does everyone in the organization have at least one key daily or weekly metric (Moneyball stat) driving his or her performance?

Rhythm—Does the organization have an effective rhythm of daily, weekly, monthly, quarterly, and annual meetings to maintain alignment and drive accountability and communication? Are the meetings well run and useful?

Jobs and Musk confirm there is only one underlying strategy to dominate your industry—what we label the "X" factor.

The "X" Factor—Identify the chokepoint/constraint in your business model and industry and then gain a 10x to 30x advantage over the competition.

For Jobs, it was locking up a proprietary Toshiba flash drive that protected the iPod from competition; and ultimately launching iTunes that allowed Apple to dominate the distribution of digital music for over a decade.

In Musk's case, his relentless focus on what he labelled his "idiot index" poised SpaceX to put more people and stuff into space, in five years, than all countries combined over 50 years for 1/30th the cost—not 30% less, but for a cost 30x less than what had previously been achieved.

To finish the triangulation, I had the opportunity to spend some time with Steve Kerr, former head of GE's famous Crotonville executive education center. I came away from that meeting with three keys to success that are useful to mid-size firms:

1. **In planning, the "middle" is gone.** You only have to define two points: where you plan to be 10 to 25 years from now and what you have to do in the next 90 days. The latter point requires real

time data and an executive team that can face the brutal reality of what the data is saying and then act accordingly. You don't want to fall in love with your own one-to-three year plans.

2. **Keep everything stupidly simple.** If your strategies, plans, decisions, systems, etc. seem complicated, they are probably wrong.
3. **All wars, and markets, are won by intelligence** — whoever has the best intel, the fastest, wins. Daily/weekly processes for gathering and acting on employee, customer, and competitor intel to feed decision making is critical.

To illustrate the first fundamental listed above; let me relate a couple decisions made by well-known entrepreneurs. Bill Gates, over forty years ago, set a very simple company vision—a computer on every desk and in every home. A decade later, feeling that this vision was so close to coming true, it was time to come up with a new one: empower people through great software—any time, any place and on any device, something Microsoft has accomplished in becoming one of the largest market cap firms on the planet. Not particularly fancy, but it's a stake in the ground that is long term.

In parallel, Tom Siebel, founder and CEO of Siebel Systems, had all employees outline their handful of objectives each quarter and post them on an internal portal for everyone to see. (Tom was the first to post and lets all employees see his priorities.) This made it crystal clear what was expected each quarter, with compensation tied to the quantifiable objectives.

Defining a simple long-term vision 10–25 years out and deciding on a handful of priorities for the next quarter are the two most important decisions a business leader makes. And it's this yin and yang of having both a long-term "rarely changes" piece alongside a short-term "changes a lot" dynamic piece that provides the delicate balance needed to drive superior performance.

One last concept and then I'll summarize this overview and give you a quick glance at each chapter. Strategos, the firm of the great business strategist Gary Hamel (among other things, he's the guru behind the notion of core competencies), provides a beautifully simple definition of strategy, which I'll paraphrase:

You don't have a real strategy if it doesn't pass these two tests: what you're planning to do really matters to your existing and potential customers; and second, it differentiates you from your competition.

Add to this the requirement that you have the ability to become the best at implementing this strategy (back to core competencies) and you have a clear idea whether you really have a strategy or not that will work. Some firms do things that differentiate themselves but it doesn't really matter to a customer (high quality when the customer just wants speed) while other firms do things that the customer desires, but so does all the competition (you've just entered the commodity zone). And yet others might have both parts of the strategy correct from a theoretical standpoint, but fail to execute. Keep this simple definition of strategy in mind as you read the rest of the book.

People, Strategy, Execution, Cash

We've organized the Scaling Up Performance Platform, and the chapters in this book, around four key decisions. They help overcome the barriers your team will face as you scaleup:

People—in leading people, take a page from parenting: Establish a handful of rules, repeat yourself a lot, and act consistently with those rules. This is the role and power of Core Values.

If discovered and used effectively, these values guide all decisions (people and process) in the company.

Strategy—in setting strategy, follow the definition from the great business strategist Gary Hamel.

You don't have a real strategy if it doesn't pass two tests: First, what you're planning to do really matters to enough customers; and second, it differentiates you from your competition.

Execution—in driving execution, implement three key habits: Set a handful of Priorities (the fewer the better); gather quantitative and qualitative Data daily and review weekly to guide decisions; and establish an effective daily, weekly, monthly, quarterly, and annual meeting *Rhythm* to keep everyone in the loop. Those who pulse faster, scale faster.

Cash—in managing cash, don't run out of it! Pay as much attention to how every decision affects cash flow as you would to revenue and profitability.

This book provides you tools for making these simple decisions and then the tools for keeping everyone aligned and accountable to those decisions. More specifically:

CHAPTER 1: "Barriers to Scale" is written differently than all the other chapters, providing a dynamic look at the three barriers to scaling a firm.

People Section

CHAPTER 2: "Right People Doing the Right Things Right" model provides an overall framework for what decisions need to be made and in what order to increase the value of your business. It aligns nicely with Jim Collins research in what it takes to make a good firm great.

CHAPTER 3: "Core Values" provide a way to keep those "rarely changed" handful of rules alive in the company.

Strategy Section

CHAPTER 4: "Brand Promise" provides a simple formula for narrowing in on the key strategy necessary to dominate your market.

CHAPTER 5: "One-Page Strategic Plan" helps you get your long-term and short-term vision, metrics, and priorities on a single page to aid communication and alignment.

CHAPTER 6: "Customer and Employee Feedback" provides the intel—real time data—needed to choose the "right" priorities and to let you know you're acting consistent to those priorities. At the end of the chapter, a brief overview of Smart Numbers and Critical Numbers will be provided.

Execution Section

CHAPTER 7: "Organizational Alignment and Focus" gets specific about the Top 5 and Top 1 of 5 approach to prioritization.

CHAPTER 8: "Quarterly Themes" shows how to place a spotlight on the number one priority to keep it top of mind.

CHAPTER 9: "Meeting Rhythms" provides specific agendas for making these vital meetings effective. Reread the various CEO endorsements if you don't think these meetings are crucial.

Cash Section

Chapter 10: "Cash Flow" replicates a chapter in our book Scaling Up because of the critical importance of maintaining positive cash flow to scaling organizations and keep from "growing broke."

Case Studies

There are hundreds of articles and case studies of firms successfully using our tools to scale to millions and billions posted on our media site *www.ScaleUps.com*. Over 102,000+ firms have used these tools to make it easier to scale.

Implementation

Most executives discover the best way to implement the tools is to purchase this book for every senior leader and team leads and go through one chapter per month discussing how the concepts can be applied to your firm. Many leaders also purchase a book for every employee (boxes of books, for less than half the cost on Amazon, available at www.scalingup.com). It's inexpensive training and provides the rest of the employees with important context for the changes the senior leaders are making. Engage a Scaling Up Certified coach to further support implementation.

Digital Forms

Editable PDFs in over 25 languages of the One-Page Strategic Plan (OPSP) document and other one-page Growth Tools can be found via a link in the opening banner of *www.ScalingUp.com*.

Keep on learning and scaling!

Verne Harnish, CEO
Scaling Up
verne@ScalingUp.com

1

BARRIERS TO SCALE

What CEOs of growing companies know that you may not—and how you can use it to build a powerhouse business

Executive Summary: There are three barriers to growth common among all growing firms: the need for the executive team to grow as leaders in their abilities to delegate and predict; the need for systems and structures to handle the complexity that comes with growth; and the need to navigate the increasingly tricky market dynamics that mark arrival in a larger marketplace.

Alan Rudy was a disillusioned CEO. "Wasn't I supposed to be making more money and having more fun, the bigger the company got?" wondered the founder of Express-Med, a mail-order medical supplies firm based in New Albany, Ohio. "I was angry all of the time," remembers Alan. "I had a long weekend planned to go skiing with my father and two brothers, for the first time in ten years, yet I backed out at the last minute because the business needed me to hold things together." To make matters worse, on March 30 of that year he was shown financials by his CFO that estimated a first-quarter profit of $300K, yet two days later, on April 1, his CFO said that they had actually *lost* $350K. Chuckles Alan today, "For several hours, I thought it was an elaborate April Fool's joke. I kept trying to be a good sport about it, yet it turned out to be true." Capping it off during that time were employees in fist-fights in the parking lot, and one employee slashing the tires of another because of something said at work. Needless to say "stress was a little high," says Alan. Yet, within two years Alan had reversed the trends and his seven-year-old firm became a $65-million winner. More importantly "It's fun again and we're making money."

Express-Med is among the elite: of all firms in the United States, only 4 percent survive the transition from a startup to a growing firm. David Birch, founder of Cognetics and the official keeper of business growth statistics, calls that 4% "gazelles," which are firms that grow at least 20% a year for four years in a row. These are not huge, old elephants that are cutting back on employees. Nor are they mice—too tiny to create more than a handful of jobs. North America's gazelles—all of which started as mere mice—now fuel more than two-thirds of the world's economic growth and essentially all of its job creation.

As the statistics indicate, becoming a gazelle—a scaleup—isn't easy, requiring the entrepreneur to navigate a specific set of challenges, any one of them potentially life-threatening to the business. The good news is that the barriers to growth are known, and the tools for handling them are within the grasp of any entrepreneur. All it takes to make growing your business both fun and profitable, at each and every stage of its life, is the discipline to find the right tools and implement them.

"It's true what they say: Routine sets you free. I don't love structure. It's just what I have to do, [if] I want to do all the things that I want to do," says Alan. "And a pulse of 200 beats a year from 300 hearts in the company, now, that's a lot of blood flowing in the right direction."

Market Dynamics

The market can make you look smart or dumb, as we've all seen over the years. Move with a trend and you win; try and buck a market movement and it can crush you. For architect Steve Smith of The Lawrence Group Companies in St. Louis, that point came about six years into his practice. Specializing in designing and building radio stations (the company also focuses in the healthcare and university arenas), Steve started witnessing the consolidation of the radio industry and felt he needed to respond in sync with the market. Yet he was going to have to think differently than his competitors, who view being an architect as a profession, not a business. "Most architects think about designing a building. We decided that we're about designing a business, and then finding people that design the buildings—which, in our case, is mostly radio station buildings."

This change of mindset, combined with the rise of the Internet at the time, another market force he embraced, allowed Smith to create a business model that led to a centrally managed network of architectural practices nationwide. This growth-oriented mode of thinking "is a differentiator for us in our profession," says Smith, "while bringing us the same challenges everyone faces with growth." Smith went further than thinking big. He conceived a set of core values in his business (see Chapter 3, Core Values) and put in the systems, metrics, and structures necessary to deal with the complexity. He's built the culture and discipline that resulted in The Lawrence Group being voted "the best place to work" in St. Louis for his size category of firms.

With growth, market pressures increase and strategic decisions come with higher stakes. At $10 million and higher, CEOs often feel their attention is being pulled inside the business just when they most need to be focusing on what's happening outside in the market. Joe McKinney of McVantage says that hard experience has taught him that growth decisions are dangerous if you don't have a good feel for what's going on both inside and outside the business.

"You have to understand where you are within your own industry and know that you've got everything handled before you try to step up to the next level, because a fall off the side of that mountain can be deadly," Joe says. "There are points along the way when you've got to get across the entire canyon to the next growth plateau in one jump. You don't get two jumps. But maybe you don't have to jump at all. Maybe the tigers on this side aren't as mean as the lions on the other side."

The plain truth is that scaling a firm can be so painful at certain stages that many otherwise successful CEO has looked to an exit strategy. Shannan Marty was sufficiently distressed with Tracer Research Group's flagging fortunes at one point that she was ready to sell—until a technological breakthrough captured the markets attention and convinced her and her partner to abandon the sale. When Express-Med went through a rough period, Alan Rudy was considering either quitting or scaling back the business to a point where it might seem fun again.

Grow Thyself

But tough times offer good CEOs the opportunity to look at themselves and their role with new eyes. Molly Wilmot of Mostly Muffins says increased managerial sophistication through executive training and coaching has allowed her to re-evaluate and re-define her role. "I've realized that my unique ability is connecting with people—selling who we are and where we're going. I don't have to manage the numbers anymore, because I have a structure doing that for me. The potential now seems endless. Now, when I think about how to grow the company, the key strategic question is, 'Who do I need to be, and what do I have to do to get there?'"

With consulting help, Alan realized he had been giving his middle managers team leaders too little authority and too many confusing instructions. He backed off, took some training to work on his personal style, and gave many of his day-to-day oversight functions to a newly hired president. Thanks to the management structures he's put in place, along with the measurements and meetings that keep it all humming, Alan was free to work on new projects and acquisitions.

"It's absolutely amazing how all of this has changed our company," he says. "Today I have time to think and try things. This is my true talent—listening to what people need, talking to competitors and customers, and adjusting my business accordingly. When I am focusing solely inside the company, I cannot move the company ahead. I am much more the CEO than I was before."

After exiting Express-Med, Rudy went on to scale several additional ventures using Scaling Up. Business is finally fun and generating returns for himself and the economy—which add to the rewards of scaling a business. This, too, is within your reach if you choose to make the leap.

Barriers to Growth

There are roughly 32 million firms in the US, of which only 6 percent get above $1 million in revenue. Of those firms, only about 1 out of 10, or 0.5 percent of *all* companies, ever make it to $10 million in revenue and only 56,000 companies surpass $100 million. Finishing out the list, the top 500 public and private firms exceed $7.2 billion (2023). Data indicate that there are similar ratios in other countries.

As organizations scale up this growth path they go through a predictable series of evolutions and revolutions *(Figure 1-1)*.

Let's review the three barriers that prevent firms from moving along this path: lack of leadership, lack of systems and structures, and market dynamics.

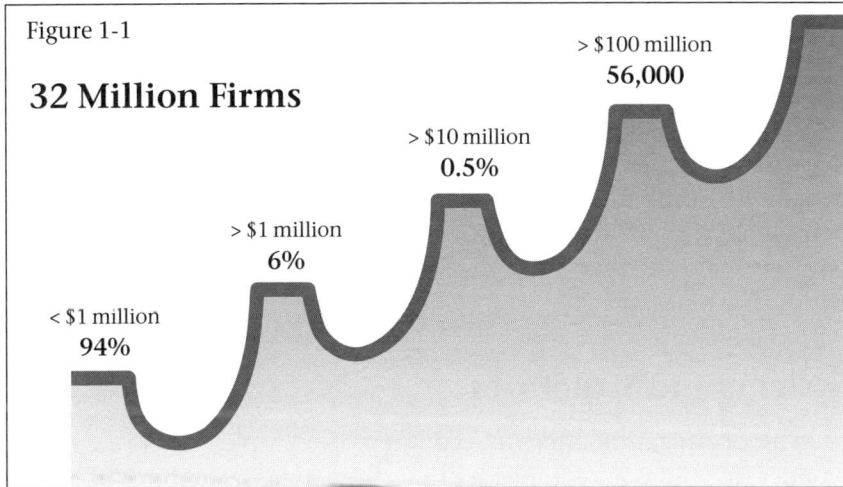

Figure 1-1

32 Million Firms

> $100 million
56,000

> $10 million
0.5%

> $1 million
6%

< $1 million
94%

Leadership

As goes the leadership team goes the rest of the firm. Whatever strengths or weaknesses exist within the organization can be traced right back to the cohesion of the executive team and their levels of trust, competence, discipline, alignment, and respect. The two most important attributes of effective leaders are their abilities to predict and to delegate. Within the category of prediction I include the ability to set a compelling strategy that anticipates market movements. Leaders don't have to be years ahead, just minutes ahead of the market, the competition, and those they lead. And the ability to accurately predict revenues and earnings is the ultimate test of leadership from the perspective of Wall Street and the public markets. AI is proving valuable in helping leaders predict.

If we look at the second attribute of effective leadership, the ability to delegate, we can understand why most firms have fewer than ten employees. Getting others to do something as good as or better than yourself is one of the hardest aspects of leadership, but necessary if you're going to scale the business. Thus, most entrepreneurs prefer to operate alone or with a couple of people. To get to the level of ten employees, the founders must at least begin to delegate those functions in which they are weak. As the organization approaches 50 employees, whatever is the strength of the top leader can become the weakness of the organization. From 50 employees up, it's then a matter of adding a layer of frontline leaders. The success of the firm is determined by the extent to which the senior leadership team can grow the next level of leadership, and teach them in turn to predict and delegate effectively.

Successful delegation starts with choosing the right person or team. Keep in mind the rule that one great person can replace three good people. With the right people, delegation is a four-step process to pinpoint what they are to do, create a measurement system for monitoring progress, provide feedback, and then give out appropriately timed recognition and reward.

Systems and Structures

As an organization grows it becomes more complex. There are mathematical formulas for complexity that show that as you move from two products, employees, or sites to four products, employees, or sites, your complexity increases by a factor of twelve. It's a force of nature: the lowly amoeba can do everything it needs with one cell, but as the number of cells increase the organism begins to develop subsystems—for feeding, elimination, circulation, procreation, etc. The same is true for companies. Increases in complexity leads to stress, miscommunications, costly errors, poor customer service, and greater overall costs.

To keep from being buried, an organization must put in place appropriate systems and structures. When you go from two employees to ten, you need better telecommunication systems and more structured space. If your company goes to 50 employees, you still need space and phones, but suddenly you need an accounting system that shows more precisely whether, which, and how projects, customers, or products are actually making money. From 50 employees (or from $10 to $50 million in revenue), typically all the information-technology systems need to be upgraded. And above $50 million, you get to revamp them again, as the organization tries to tie all systems to one database of customers and employees.

Considering structures, as the firm grows it becomes increasingly important to pay attention to organizational-structure issues. The key is to think in terms of three types of organizational charts. The first looks like what most of us know as the standard hierarchical organizational chart. I call it an accountability chart. The second type is actually a set of organizational charts that map work process or work flow. The third, the Almost Matrix, maps the relationships between organizational functions and the various business units that begin to form as the organization grows.

Accountability charts: A company will often become stuck or experience a lot of miscommunications and balls getting dropped when there isn't clear accountability established within an organization. All projects, line items on an income statement, priorities, and processes must ultimately be owned by a single person, even though there might be hundreds of people who have some kind of sub-accountabilities and responsibilities in seeing something completed. Elon Musk is fanatical about making sure every activity and decision has a single person accountable (please read Walter Isaacson's biography of Elon Musk).

There are two basic rules accompanying the creation of an accountability chart. First, there can be no "to be determined's" on the chart. If you can conceive of a position, put someone's name in it, even if his or her only accountability is to make sure the position is filled. Organizations often place the term "acting" in front of the title of someone filling a spot until it can be permanently filled.

Second, there are always a few people in the organization who shouldn't be leading other people, yet are considered senior in the organization. In this case, a few "off org chart" positions are advisable.

Work process charts: Because the accountability chart can't capture all the interactions necessary to run a business without a mass of dotted lines running all over the chart, it's better to keep the accountability chart clean and then establish four to nine work flow charts representing the critical processes/value drivers that flow through the organization. These processes might include how you acquire a customer, how a project moves through the organization, how employees are selected and trained, and how customers are billed and payments collected. It's advisable to take the one process per quarter that seems the most dysfunctional and clean it up. Processes are like garages and hallway closets, which become messed up over time and require regular attention.

Almost Matrix: This chart shows the relationships between organizational functions and the business units that form as the organization grows. These units begin to feel and act like separate businesses within the business. They can be organized around product lines, customer niches, geographical locations, or business units acting as wholly owned subsidiaries of the parent company. Conflicts often arise between the functional leaders, like the VP of Sales and Marketing, and the business unit heads who have sales people driving their revenue. The key question is, to whom do the sales people report in the organization? This kind of tension often leads to a regular cycle of centralizing and then de-centralizing certain functions within the organization, which can consume a lot of energy. Our position is that most people should be accountable to the business unit leaders; the role of the functional leader is one of coaching and bringing best practices into the organization. It's a complex issue that requires some real thought and expertise.

Overall, it's important to think in terms of multiple organizational charts and to assign accountability to someone to make sure the various charts are being updated. In my book *Scaling Up (Rockefeller Habits 2.0)*, there are some new one-page tools called the Function Accountability Chart (FACe) and the Process Accountability Chart (PACe).

Market Dynamics

The market makes you look either smart or dumb. When it's going your way, it covers up a lot of mistakes. When fortunes reverse, all your weaknesses seem to be exposed. And there's a counter-intuitive aspect of growing a business: when the firm is under $10 million in revenue and just a little more focus internally on establishing healthy organizational habits would pay off in the long run, you have a tendency to focus mostly externally. In turn, as the organization passes $10 million, the organizational complexity issues start drawing the attention of the senior team inward at a time when it's probably more important for the team to be focused more on the marketplace. This is when it's useful to have outside assistance in dealing with internal issues so you can remain focused externally.

Going back to the evolution and revolution chart and considering the basic measures of a business—revenue, gross margin, profit, and cash—there is an important sequence of things to focus on. Between start-up and the first million or two in revenue, the key driver is revenue. The focus is on getting the marketplace interested in you.

As for cash, the entrepreneur relies on self-funding or friends, family, and fools in the very beginning.

Between $1 million and $10 million, you add to your focus on revenue the cash concerns you had been putting off. Since the organization will typically grow more and faster during this stage than any other, you risk "growing broke" with cash being rapidly consumed. In addition, in this stage the organization is experimenting a great deal to figure out what its specific focus and position in the market should be. These experiments can be costly.

As the organization passes $10 million, internal and external pressures come to the forefront. Externally, the organization is on more radar screens, alerting competitors to your threats. Customers are beginning to demand lower prices as they do more business with your organization. At the same time, internal complexities increase, which cause costs to rise faster than revenue. All of this begins to squeeze an organization's gross margin. As gross margin slips a few points the organization is starved of the extra money it needs to invest in infrastructure like accounting systems and training, creating a snowball effect as the organization passes the $25-million mark. It's now critical that the company maintains a clear value proposition in the market to prevent price erosion. At the same time the company must continually simplify and automate internal processes to reduce costs. Organizations successful at doing both can actually see their gross margins increase during this stage of growth.

By $50 million in revenue an organization is expected to have enough experience and position in the marketplace that it can accurately predict profitability. Not that profit hasn't been important all along as the organization grows. It's just more critical at this stage that an organization can *predict* profitability, since a few point swings either way represents millions of dollars.

This brings us full circle to the number one function of a leader, the ability to predict. The fundamental journey of a growing business is to create a *predictable* engine in an unpredictable world.

In summary, growing a business is a dynamic process that requires a shifting set of priorities as the leadership team navigates the predictable evolutions and revolutions of growth. Continuing to grow the capabilities of leadership throughout the organization; installing systems and structures to handle increasing complexities; and capitalizing on the market dynamics that impact the business, are fundamental to successfully scaling a business that's fun and profitable.

Start to Scale

PEOPLE

2

RIGHT PEOPLE DOING THE RIGHT THINGS RIGHT

Optimize Your Human Capital!

Executive Summary: This chapter provides an overall framework for the three key decisions that drive the value of your business. They align nicely with Jim Collins' 25 years of research in what it takes to make a good firm great.

There are three basic decisions an executive team must make:

1. Do we have the Right People?
2. Are we doing the Right Things?
3. Are we doing those Things Right?

The Right People

Fortune magazine surprised the business world by choosing The Container Store as the #1 "Best Companies to Work For," beating out standards like Southwest Airlines, GE, Microsoft and SAS. A 25-store retail chain at the time, it sells products that help you organize your home and was launched by Kip Tindell and Garrett Boone. If you go to their website, www.containerstore.com, and click on Careers, you'll see their hiring philosophy. In essence, they firmly believe that one great person can replace three good people.

They also pay their people 50 to 100 percent more than typical retailers, which can be done if you have proportionately fewer people, and provides them with over 200 hours of training their first year versus the ten hours standard in the retail industry. Not two to three times the amount of training, but over twenty times the amount of training. And, again, this isn't a Silicon Valley tech firm. This is a company in the tough retail business sector.

Obviously, a key to The Container Store's success is that they have the Right People. And their formula is simple; fewer people, paid more and given lots of training and development. Worried about spending all that money on training people so they can go elsewhere? The research is definitive that training and development increases loyalty. Besides, what's the alternative? Do you really want a bunch of untrained people scaling your business?

The first question you must ask is "Do I have the Right People?" And a quick way to discern the answer is to ask yourself if you would enthusiastically rehire each person on your team if given the opportunity. It's a question Scott Farquhar, retired co-CEO of Atlassian, considers the most important HR question.

The second question to ask, especially regarding your executive team and other key employees, is whether you think they have the potential to be the best in their position three to five years from now. (By the way, you might have the Right People, just in the wrong position.) When you have "A" players in every position, it makes all the difference in the world.

Hiring—Selling the Vision

Books have been written exclusively on the subject of hiring. (I'll mention an important one later in this chapter). However, there are a few basics to hiring that can go a long way toward making sure you're getting the right people. The first is to understand that hiring is a numbers game. The firms that get the best people tend to get a lot of people applying for each position and the general quality of the applicant pool is so high, throwing a dart at the list of potential employees will likely land you a great hire. This is why a firm with a stellar reputation in its industry (or even in a particular town if you hire locally) is able to continue to hire stellar people.

So, ask yourself the question: did we get a lot of high-quality people to apply for the last position we hired, especially if it was an executive position? This applies whether you used a headhunting firm (do they have access to a large pool of quality applicants?) or you're driving the process yourself. You or your headhunter should source an initial pool of 50 high-quality people to choose from. If you're relying on your network of contacts to find someone, are you reasonably sure they are in contact with a large pool of high-quality people? Remember, "A-Player" people tend to surround themselves with "A Player" people, so go only to your "A-Player" network of friends. I'm very serious about this recommendation.

A useful tool for recruiting a high-quality pool of applicants to fill executive positions, is to make a Top 10 list. Take out a piece of paper and write down at least 10 people (20 is best) you could e-mail tomorrow who have contact with the kind of A-Player talent you want to hire. Then email them a two-paragraph summary describing your firm, the position, and type of person you're seeking. Make it a point to call the people on your list as quickly as possible and let them know you're sending the summary by e-mail. Follow-up a week later to see if they know anyone or if they at least know someone who might know someone. This, by the way, is essentially what headhunters do, so if you're unwilling to do this, hire a headhunter.

Another important basic for hiring, whether you're sending out an e-mail, placing ads, using a headhunter, or utilizing several of the online job services like Indeed, is to make sure you're truly selling the company and its vision. You need to market your firm to potential employees with the same vigor you use to attract potential customers. As shown in the following example, I had a client that simply changed their ad from the first one to the second one and increased the number of applicants three-fold:

EMPLOYMENT AD—Exceptional opportunity! Rapidly growing promotional marketing agency with Fortune 500 clients seeking: ACCOUNT EXECUTIVE (description only delineating qualifications).

versus

WHEN WAS THE LAST TIME YOU HAD FUN AT WORK? It's a great time to join our promotional marketing agency team. Get all the benefits of working with Fortune 500 clients in a small-agency environment. Not only do we take pride in what we do, we have FUN. Your creativity & energy are what we need. PROMOTIONS MANAGER description (delineating what you'll do) and ACCOUNT EXECUTIVE description. Enjoy coming to work. Send resume to _____.

If using a headhunter, work with them to create a persuasive description of the company and position they can share.

Last, for frontline and first line leadership talent, your best source is referrals from you're existing A-player employees. The key is to offer significant referral bonuses—$5000 vs. $500. Pay 10% of the bonus when the referral is hired; 40% at their sixth month anniversary; and the last 50% when it's been a year.

The Selection Process

Interviewing is the most perilous part of the process because there is actually a slight negative correlation between who you likely hire based on an interview and whether they would be a great fit with your firm. Given how badly many people conduct interviews, again, you would be better off throwing a dart at the final list of candidates! The only interview process that is effective is a structured interview. Brad and Geoff Smart are the experts in this field. I highly recommend their books *Foolproof Hiring* and *Who: The A Method for Hiring*.

Testing is considerably more accurate and objective than the standard feel-good interview and should always supplement the interview process. Many of the best-run firms have their applicants, especially potential executives or frontline leaders, submit to several hours of formal testing. Least important of the tests, though the one everyone seems to use, is the standard personality test.

No time for amateur hour when utilizing testing—use professionals to help with this process. My firm recommends to all clients Bartell & Bartell, (814-861-6606) for leader and executive hires. It will cost you roughly $600 per candidate, so we recommend doing the testing on the top three picks. And you'll need to have yourself tested so they can check for compatibility. For the rest of your hires we recommend Bigby Havis & Associates' online testing products (972-233-6055). Again, you need to have yourself tested.

Will, Values, Results, Skills

You're looking for four attributes in hiring. First, do they have will—the will to learn, the will to persevere, the will to win? Second, do they fit your culture by aligning with your values (see Chapter 3, Core Values)? Third, can they achieve the results you're seeking i.e. bring in $10 million in revenue? And last, do they have the skills you're seeking?

We've written a book entitled *The Habits of Valuable Employees* which further delineates these four attributes and is a useful book for every employee to read in helping you scale your organization. It will give them the tools to help them become more valuable to the organization and themselves.

In addition to using Brad and Geoff Smart's Topgrading interview process to discern whether a candidate has these four attributes, I recommend and use a variation of an assessment-center approach. Outline on a piece of paper three or four business challenges you're expecting candidates to face when hired and then give them 30 minutes to an hour to work through how they would handle each. Then spend another 30-minutes working through their solutions with them to see how they think and to get a sense how you might work together. If nothing else, when I've employed this technique I've picked up even from the candidates I've not hired some great insights into business challenges I'm facing. One time I even contracted with a candidate to do a special project, even though the candidate knew I wasn't offering a permanent position.

Though not always possible, the best way to select the Right Person is to have someone work with you for several weeks doing the work you're expecting him or her to do. For frontline hires, "temp-to-perm" placement firms are popular because they allow you to test-drive the candidate. For management hires, see if they can work with you in the evenings on a consulting basis. Several of my venture capital friends have found, especially when hiring a top executive, that nothing substitutes for simply working alongside the final candidate over an extended period of time dealing with the tough issues facing the business. Google's founders Larry Page and Sergey Brin put Eric Schmidt on their board for almost a year before putting him in the CEO position. That's why promoting from within and hiring people you've worked with in the past are so effective.

Overall, getting the right people in the right positions is the first and most important job of the CEO and executive team. Also important is getting the wrong people out as quickly as possible—though for many reasons this is one of the hardest aspects of running a business. It's why you need a strong executive team and a top-notch coach so they can alert you when you're blind to the obvious facts. Often you just can't see the problematic people yourself.

Right Things Right Model

The Right Things Right model *(Figure 2-1)* illustrates the fundamental decisions, relationships and functions of a business. The three ovals on the left side of the model show the Right Things; the three ovals on the right show how to do Things Right. Every business theory can be mapped onto the model; it provides a framework with which to integrate various business theories. It's also a useful model to help explain to all employees the fundamentals of business. Lastly, it serves as a useful tool for choosing quarterly priorities.

The key questions on the Right Things side of the model are "Do you have a viable economic model?" Or, more bluntly, can you ever make real money doing what you're doing? Do you have a product or service that enough customers value to make a viable business? And have you determined the X factor that you can control that differentiates you from the competition, matters to customers and provides you an advantage in the marketplace? Can you be the best in your chosen sandbox?

The key questions on the Things Right side of the model are "Do you have the management practices and processes to take advantage of the market opportunity you're pursuing?" Do you have the habits and disciplines in place to maintain your competitive advantage? Is your organization structured properly to maximize the productivity of the employees? Can you deliver a consistent service or product offering?

Moving down through the model, you know you're doing the Right Things when revenue or market share—or both—are growing at twice the market. Though most executives feel their business is unique, you can always approximate the growth of your industry segment from various sources. And if your industry segment is in decline, are you growing at least twice as fast as your nearest competitor as you divide up what's left as others exit the market?

The Right Things side requires bold leadership able to make a few key decisions about strategy and direction, especially when the business needs to make an abrupt turn in the market—like Facebook's decision to pivot from desktop to mobile as they were going public. The Things Right side requires capable management that can maintain healthy disciplines and habits. Interestingly, much of what is good management is being augmented by and will eventually be replaced by technology/generative AI so that the people in the organization can focus more on leading instead of managing. Our firm has created some

Figure 2-1

Right Things Right

Lead People   Manage Activities

Reputation   **Productivity**

Get, Keep, Grow   **Better, Faster, Cheaper**

executive management automation systems that are already heading down this path (we have a SaaS platform called Align/Scoreboard).

If you then consider that a business is simply "people" doing "activities," the model supports a familiar notion that you lead people and manage their activities—you don't manage people. Think of the parenting approach that says you love the child while being tough on their inappropriate behaviors, i.e. "son, you're good, what you did is bad" versus "son, you're bad." It's important to separate the person from their activities. While continuing to inspire people through your leadership skills, you must also be diligent about holding people accountable to results. In fact, you might have to love someone enough to let him or her go. (I tend to prefer the phrase "freeing up your future!")

This is where the model gets more explicit. The Right Things side represents the people and relationships involved in any business; the Things Right side represents the activities or transactions that occur within a business to deliver consistent products and services to the market. The three fundamental groups of people that interact in a business are Customers, Employees (including suppliers and sub-contractors), and Shareholders—which models closely the *Balanced Scorecard* system UPS and other firms have adopted. (There's a book called *The Balanced Scorecard* for those interested—it essentially supports the notion that a leader's success is defined as having satisfied all three stakeholders, not just one or two.)

The three fundamental activities at the heart of all businesses are the functions of Making or Buying something, Selling something, and Keeping Good Records. This mirrors the primary top executive functions of COO (make or buy), VP Sales and Marketing (sell), and CFO (records), with the CEO serving as their leader. Though the titles may vary, it's this fundamental troika serving under the CEO that makes an effective organization.

Taking the model further, on the Right Things side you strive to achieve three outcomes: get, keep and grow all three relationships. To do this, you need to figure out what basic needs (jobs to be done) you can fill for a certain group of customers in a way that differentiates you from the competition and then what competencies your people need to meet those needs so that value is created for the shareholders. I was specific in using the term "needs" versus "wants." Customers can bankrupt you with their wants, wants, wants while a laser-focused competitor can come along and deliver on a more important need and steal your customers. Ultimately, this boils down to one overarching concept—the fundamental need to build a great reputation with all three stakeholders. You know you have a great reputation when it gets easier, instead of harder, to get, keep, and grow each of the three relationships.

On the Things Right side, the organization strives to achieve three additional outcomes: doing each of the activities better, faster, and cheaper. The primary objective is to increase your gross margin percentage (a key driver of valuation) by continuing to lower the costs of delivering your products or services relative to the sales price and improving the value proposition so you can maintain your prices relative to the competition to increase profitability. The right side of the model encapsulates the classic, "buy low, sell high, and keep good records" fundamentals of business.

Looking at the Right Things Right model from a pure accounting perspective, the left side of the model represents the balance sheet of the business, delineating who owes and who owns what. The bottom line of a balance sheet is net worth—a measure of value created for the shareholders. The right side of the model represents the income statement (P&L), delineating the revenues and expenses with a bottom line of profitability.

The six circles of the Right Things Right model balance on the vision of the company, as represented by the Planning Pyramid shown at the bottom of Figure 2-1. This will be covered in Chapter 6, One-Page Strategic Plan. It's the vision of the company, from its core values to its specific accountabilities, that gives a focus to the specifics of each of the six circles—exactly who are the customers, employees, and shareholders, and exactly what are the activities in which the business will engage. What's important to note at this point is that there is a constant balancing act between the left and right sides of the model; between driving revenue and making sure the business is profitable; between having enough people and having enough activities for those people; between protecting the reputation of the firm and increasing the productivity of the firm. Business is a constant process of balancing priorities, which is why the top part of the model balances on the pinpoint vision of the company.

Putting the Model to Work

In addition to a general framework for business, there are three specific uses of the model relative to the three Scaling Up disciplines:

Discipline # 1—Priorities

A starting point to figuring out the number one priority for any particular quarter is to consider the six circles as potential priorities and choose the one on each side that needs the most attention at that moment. Be sure to specify whether the left-side driver is get, keep, or grow, and whether the right-side driver is better, faster, or cheaper. As an example, this quarter the top priority might be "increase by 25 percent (grow) the business we're doing with our top four customers" (choosing the Customers circle on the left) and "reduce the time by 50 percent (faster) it takes to properly bill our clients" (choosing the Keep Good Records circle on the right).

Even though your firm may have issues within all six areas, you can only advance one of the areas on each side at a time. And because they are all interconnected, by giving momentum to one you provide momentum to all. Selecting a specific area is one of the tougher disciplines to maintain because the tendency is to try and work on all the areas simultaneously.

Leaders find that when they focus everyone's energies around one area, it gets fixed much more quickly. Two visual analogies are helpful. First, think of the six circles as spinning plates on sticks, like you might have seen on an old Ed Sullivan rerun. At any one time, one of the plates of the three on either side is spinning slower than the other two and needs your attention.

Another way to think of the six circles is as balls being juggled in the air. As a juggler moves the balls higher and higher, he or she does it one ball at a time. The same situation applies to growing a business. It's a process of hiring employees, rounding up customers, then making sure you have cash to support the growth, as you hire more employees.... The process is never-ending.

In addition, it's very important to be clear about who is accountable for each circle in the model. Who is accountable for getting customers? Who is accountable for keeping shareholders happy? Who is accountable for making sure the sales engine (the Sell circle) is functioning properly? Going through each of the six circles and their drivers (get, keep, grow, and better, faster, cheaper) and making sure the accountabilities are clear is one of the more powerful and aligning activities I've worked on with executive teams.

Discipline #2—Data

To monitor the progress of the business daily and weekly, and to accurately predict how the next few months are likely to turn out, you need metrics for all six areas of the business. For mid-market firms, the weakness on the left side of the model is having the same kind of accurate and timely feedback from customers that you demand from accounting. On the right side of the model, mid-market firms tend to be weak in having accurate sales funnel data, primarily because the sales side of the organization tends to resist measurement, except for the top line.

Discipline #3—Rhythm

In figuring out with whom you need to have various weekly meetings, the six circles provide guidance. On the right side of the model, it's crucial that operations, sales, and accounting each has its own daily and weekly rhythms. In turn, it's important that the executive team have some rhythm in terms of meeting with customers and employees. And if you are a public company, you have an entire new set of rhythms that revolve around the shareholder circle.

Organizational Structure

The six circles provide guidance for the changing organizational structure necessary to handle growth. Around $10-million in revenue, the three fundamental functions represented by the three circles on the right begin to split. The Sell circle splits into separate sales and marketing functions, requiring different personalities to head up each. (As a side note, the key measurable for marketing or business development is lead generation.) The Make or Buy circle splits into separate operations and R&D functions (or their equivalents—all firms should have some form of R&D). And the Keep Good Records circle splits into separate accounting and finance departments. On the left side of the model, growing firms tend to develop more specific functional areas focusing on employees, (HR is the old term); focusing on customers, whereby the organization starts to create customer-focused teams to complement possible product-focused teams; and focusing on shareholders where public firms develop specific shareholder-relations departments.

In summary, the Right People Doing the Right Things Right model encompasses the fundamental decisions leaders must make to successfully drive any business. The rest of the book provides specific tools for addressing each of these areas.

3

CORE VALUES

Use core values to parent a great company!

Executive Summary: Have a few rules, repeat yourself a lot, and act in ways that are consistent with the rules—these are the three keys whether you're providing your children with a good moral foundation or providing a company with a strong cultural foundation. And the evidence is irrefutable that a strong culture leads to superior performance, higher employee retention, and a better-aligned organization. Equally important, a strong culture driven by a handful of rules (core values) makes leading people much easier, reduces the need for stacks of policies and procedures, gives everyone a framework from which to make tough decisions, and generally brings simplicity and clarity to many of these "people" systems within a firm. This chapter provides a simple exercise for discovering your core values if they've not yet been delineated, and eight actions for bringing your core values alive. You'll see how to use your core values to replace a number of random lists for organizing employee orientation, recruiting, interviewing, and performance management.

In building Verifone from $30 million to $600 million to dominate the global market of clearing credit card transactions, Hatim Tyabji said his key leadership and management tool was a booklet that explained, in eight languages, the eight core values at the heart of Verifone's success. "I essentially spent the last six years repeating myself," noted Tyabji, as he built a strong, global culture on the foundation of these eight rules.

Finding the Right Words: Mission to Mars

If you already have your core values articulated, skip to the next section. For those who haven't, read on. If you go at it cold, with a blank sheet of paper, figuring out your company's core values can be a frustrating and fruitless process. I've seen firms spend tens of thousands of dollars and several months going through a laborious collaborative process, only to come away with a generic list that misses the uniqueness and power of the existing culture. Alternatively, there is a way to get at your core values that's fun and amazingly fast. It's an approach first suggested by Jim Collins. Using the method I'm about to describe, companies can get a good first draft of their core values in 30-minutes and a finished document in a couple hours. Jim Collins refers to the process as the Mission to Mars.

Gather a representative group of employees or leaders from across the company, or if you'd rather, your senior leadership team. Ask the group to pretend there's a team of Martian anthropologists studying American business, and they're trying to understand your company's corporate culture. Each individual is to come up with the names of five employees—ones who aren't in the room—to send to Mars. (Note: If you're a start-up, your list is likely the four or five initial founders or employees. That's fine.) The Martians don't speak English, and they don't know what a good PowerPoint presentation is, so whatever the Martians learn will have to come through observation. Given that, which five employees would best convey the good things about your company, just through their actions? Don't choose people because they know how to present well, nor eliminate someone because I mentioned this. Don't over-engineer by choosing a balanced team that represents each function in the business. Just choose the five who would best give the Martians a sense of what's good about the company. To make it really simple, who are your favorite people in the company!

When each individual has five names—no more, no less—go around the room and determine the top three vote getters. Important side note: Don't let these lists out of the room. This is a thought experiment and the conversations around the three individuals chosen should stay in the room. Starting with the employee who received the most mentions, initiate a conversation about these people. Who are they? How do they go about their work? What would customers or co-workers say about them? Why are they important or valuable to the organization?

Another approach is to go the opposite direction—ask people to recall employees who didn't work out and brainstorm about what went wrong.

As you jot down what's being said, you'll begin to see themes and patterns emerge. Don't be surprised if the words that pop up are less polished or humanitarian than you might have hoped, and for Pete's sake, don't squelch those who utter them! Your goal is to know what the real core values of your organization are, not the Chamber of Commerce's notion of what they should be. Here's what Collins says about it:

...there is no universally right set of core values. A company need not have as its core value customer service (Sony doesn't) or respect for the individual (Disney doesn't) or quality (Wal-Mart Stores doesn't) or market focus (HP doesn't) or teamwork (Nordstrom doesn't). A company might have operating practices and business strategies around those qualities without having them at the essence of its being. Furthermore, great companies need not have likable or humanistic core values, although many do. The key is not what core values an organization has but that it has core values at all.

As you get closer to finding the right phrases and ideas to describe your company's core values, the energy level of the room will begin to rise. How will you know you've arrived? The goose bumps on your arm will tell you. You'll recognize your company's core values when you hear your employees stating some of your own deepest beliefs and motivations as their own. Then it takes little more than some word-smithing to get the concepts hammered into key phrases and rules that you can use. At Scaling Up, we have five:

1. Create Ecstatic Clients
2. Honor Intellectual Creatives
3. Everyone an Entrepreneur
4. Practice What We Preach
5. Relentless Transparency

The Mission to Mars exercise is powerful and revealing. I remember working through it with one of the companies in our Master of Business Dynamics program. The CEO had brought a relatively large management group to the meeting; there were probably 14 people around his table, out of the 120 total employees. The group quickly selected its five emissaries, but most of the proposed core values they put up on the board left the CEO restless. That is, until three words came into play: build, elegance, and design. You could see the synapses firing in this young CEO's brain. The word "build" took him back to his childhood, to working on projects with his dad, and it so happens that his company today provides software solutions to the construction industry. "Elegance" and "design" spoke to the impatience his employees know so well when he's confronted with a solution that seems clunky. The words resonated for him, and he seemed touched to know that they also rang true for his senior leadership team.

What happened to that software company on that day was important for its future, and that's because the communication went both ways. His leaders demonstrated that they knew the words that motivated their CEO, and the CEO gave them additional information with which to understand the deeper meaning of those words. Is it important for an organization and its CEO to understand one another in this way? Yes, absolutely. If the organization doesn't understand and starts to drift, the CEO loses his edge—maybe even gives up and sells. If the organization does understand, however, alignment happens and the company thrives.

For a great example of core values, and how to share them with your employees, clients, and the world, Google "Atlassian Core Values." You'll see a short video and a list of their five core values. Notice that each is a phrase, not a single word—and that they've used language (a little of it spicey) that fits their style and culture. You'll also see each core value anchored with a visual image. Last, look bottom right on the landing page and you'll see Atlassian using these core values as part of their recruiting and selection process.

As co-founder Scott Farquhar notes, after discovering their core values during a two-day workshop with me in Sydney in 2005, "a lot has changed since we've scaled from 50 to over 10,000 employees, but what hasn't changed are our five core values."

Techniques for Bringing Your Core Values Alive

Once you have your values, the other 99 percent of the effort goes into keeping these values alive with existing employees and inculcating (bringing into the culture) new employees and acquisitions as they join the firm. It's the repeating of and living consistent with the firm's values that's the most difficult part of the process. A leader must go beyond merely posting the values on the wall and handing out plastic laminated cards. To keep things fresh, you have to get a little creative. You have to find lots of different ways to deliver the same information— over and over—so that it doesn't get stale yet is reinforced on a daily basis.

Storytelling

Everybody enjoys a good story and most great leaders teach through parables or storytelling. While this provides that spoonful of sugar that helps the medicine go down, there's more to it than that. As I saw when I did the Mission to Mars exercise with my MBD client, a little bit of story and legend helps cement the bond between the CEO and employee. It keeps the CEO interested and involved. Above all, the story provides the explanation for any core values that might seem unusual or cryptic on their own. You can tell the story and, instead of offering a moral, you can say "and that's why we consider (blank) one of our core values."

The Mission to Mars exercise is an ideal time to start a tradition of corporate storytelling, but don't stop there. Incorporate storytelling wherever it logically fits into your management strategy. Tell the oldest stories when you can, but also encourage the telling of new stories. The more that employees are able to attach core values to incidents in their working lives, the more relevant and useful those core values become.

To get storytelling into your routine, start by making it a practice at your monthly or quarterly all-employee meetings (you do have them, don't you?) by sharing a story from the past month or quarter that represents each core value. The quickest way to come up with these stories is to take 15-minutes at one of your weekly executive team meetings (you do have those, don't you?) and ask for nominations and examples. If you're among those who haven't yet established a routine of having all-employee and executive-team meetings regularly, read Chapter 9, Meeting Rhythm.

Recruitment and Selection

Once you've established the words, rules, and stories that constitute your core values, put them to work in the recruitment and selection of employees. It's critical for new employees to feel comfortable in your culture, and the best way to determine that is to ensure that they align with your core values. Start by using the language from your core values in recruitment ads and job descriptions. This will catch the attention of those people who resonate with those values. When it comes time to interview, design several of your questions and assessments to test the candidates' alignment with your core values. For instance, we look for people with an entrepreneurial background (Everyone an Entrepreneur). Then, when it comes time to make a selection, have the various interviewers involved rate the candidate in terms of his or her perceived alignment with each core value. Your goal, after all, is to make sure your new hires fit in. The way to improve the chances of their fitting in is by making judgments about their ability to adopt your core values as their own.

Orientation

Once hired, it's time to inculcate the individual. Like many social organization initiations, orientation (you do have one, don't you?) is when you can further emphasize the company's core values.

Courtney Dickinson, formerly Sapient's Culture Architect, established a week-long Boot Camp, in which a primary goal was to assist computer-trained techies to function in a customer-supportive environment. She used Sapient's core values to organize the experiential learning, and she found it uncommonly powerful. "I wish I had these core values to show my former employer, so they'd know why I left," one employee told her, "because this is what I believe." Dickinson says Boot Camp was optional at first—but not for long. "Just about everybody who didn't do Boot Camp was soon gone," she recalls. "It had a huge impact on retention."

At a minimum, have the CEO or other top executive come into orientation and share a company legend behind each core value. This will be reinforcing for all concerned.

Performance Appraisal

Just as core values should be the outline for your selection and orientation process, they should also be the skeleton on which you hang your performance-appraisal system. With a little creativity, any performance measure can be made to link with a core value.

In addition, organize your employee handbook into sections around each core value. There isn't a HR policy that can't fit within one of your core values.

Recognition and Reward

When you're looking for recognition and reward categories, look no further than your core values. Using them publicly—at quarterly or annual meetings or on a good-news bulletin board—reinforces the primacy of these core values within your organization. You also gain a new source of corporate stories and legends each time a reward or recognition is given that highlights a core value. For instance, at our quarterly planning session we'll often recognize someone who exemplified the "Practice What We Preach" or "Honor Intellectual Creatives" core value.

Internal Newsletter

Why struggle to come up with a catchy title for a newsletter when some word or phrase from your core values will do beautifully? Why organize your newsletter around seasons or quarters or heaven-knows-what, when you've got built-in themes in your core values? Highlight a core value with each issue, incorporating stories—yes, more stories—about people putting these core values to work for the betterment of the company.

Themes

I know I'm starting to sound a bit like a broken record here, but your core values are the most obvious source of quarterly or annual themes. Use your core values to bring attention to your corporate improvement efforts. Milliken, the textile manufacturer, takes one of its six core values and makes it the theme for the quarter, asking all employees to focus on ways to improve the company around the theme. The Ritz-Carlton chain goes to the other extreme and highlights one rule every day, in locations worldwide. In either case, a rhythm has been established that keeps the core values in sight and in mind simply by repetition. As part of that process, you might even ask your employees to audit the firm as to its alignment (or nonalignment) with a particular core value. Such an effort does far more than reinforce the core value—it can produce some very healthy and needed dialogue. That's the sort of thing that keeps core values from being just a list on the wall.

Everyday Management

I've found that leaders and CEOs can repeat core values endlessly without it seeming ridiculous—so long as the core values they're using are relevant and meaningful to their employees. When you make a decision, relate it to a core value. When you reprimand or praise, refer to a core value. When customer issues arise, by all means compare the situation to the ideal represented by the core values. The same goes for employee beefs and concerns—weigh them against your company's core values. Small as these actions may sound, they probably do more than any of the aforementioned strategies for bringing core values alive in your organization.

Have a Few Rules, Repeat Yourself, and Be Consistent

As you move forward discovering and bringing alive your core values, remember: this is no different than teaching your two-year-old right from wrong. Young, old, or in-between: people need to know what marks they're supposed to be hitting. They want to understand how they can conduct themselves to please you and your customers. They appreciate a reminder when they goof up. And they want to know the rules aren't a moving target or prone to selective enforcement. Your core values will do all of that for you, if you take the time to find out what they are and how you can best make use of them.

Now, in a growing environment, it may be tempting to say, "We don't have time to slow down and figure out things like core values!" But I've coached scores of companies over the years and I'll tell you, every company on a rocket, every company that's gaining sales and influence in quantum leaps, takes the time.

Core Value Checklist

ACTIVITY: In this column, list someone **accountable** for taking action on each item you want to pursue. Also, go to One-Page Strategic Plan and fill out Core Value column.

Have a few rules, repeat yourself, and be consistent.

Create Legends—Link a company story with each core value to make it memorable. Storytelling is the best way to teach. Do this now, while you're together.

Recruitment and Selection—Use the core values in your ads and selection process. Have them serve as the section themes or headings for your structured interview process.

Orientation—Have your core values serve as the major themes for your orientation process.

Appraisal Process—Have your core values serve as the section headings for your appraisal process. With a little creativity, any performance measure can be made to link with a core value.

Recognition and Reward—At the quarterly or annual company gathering, if you're looking for recognition and reward categories, look no further than your core values. And this serves to generate new stories to bring them alive.

Internal Newsletter—Each issue, highlight a core value with an example of someone exemplifying the value.

Themes—Whether as a theme for a particular round of good news stories or as a company-wide quarterly theme, use the core values to bring focus to improvement efforts. Ask people to take time to audit the firm along the lines of a core value. It produces some very healthy and often dialogue that is often needed, and needed often.

Everyday Management—Without going to the ridiculous (though it's hard to repeat yourself enough), relate decisions, reprimands, praise, customer issues, and employee concerns back to the core values. These daily actions will do more than any of the other strategies to strengthen the culture within the firm.

Start to Scale

STRATEGY

4

CUSTOMER AND EMPLOYEE FEEDBACK

De-hassle your organization!

Executive Summary: Recurrent customer and employee hassles cost your employees 40 percent of their time, not to mention what it's costing your company in lost customers and revenues. To address, construct a system of customer and employee feedback/intel to figure out which problems (opportunities in disguise) are arising and recurring in your organization or with your customers. This chapter provides a bridge between People and the rest of the book since feedback from customers and employees needs to inform both your Strategy and Execution decisions.

What causes people to be less engaged at work? What makes them non-productive, complaint-happy deadwood? One answer: recurring problems and hassles—situations, problems, and mistakes that happen over and over again, with no resolution.

Recurring problems and hassles are worse for customers, who don't have any incentive (like salary) to hang around.

Don't get me wrong: People like a challenge. When problems crop up in ones and twos, we gear up to perform. Struggling to find a solution can be exhilarating, even affirming. Solving customer problems is at the heart of business and can actually build loyalty and lead to new opportunities. But recurring problems are something else entirely. They're like water on a rock, wearing your organization down day after day, leaving associates and customers frustrated.

Recurring problems eat up more than 40 percent of the average employee's time. Why so much? Because a problem is rarely just one person's concern. And addressing the issue often brings a process or progress to a halt.

To reduce your costs, shorten your cycle time, and generally improve your internal working environment, systematically gather data on what's hassling your customers and employees—and then *do* something about it. And because your employees are often closest to the customer, their hassles are usually related to what's hassling your customers, giving you tremendous insight into ways to serve your customers better. Their hassles are your opportunities.

Almost four decades ago, when Dell Computer was just a baby called PCs Limited, Michael had his employees keep weekly lists. He urged them to write down every problem, complaint, concern, issue, idea, or suggestion that had either crossed their minds or had been reported by a customer that week. On Thursday afternoons these lists were turned in, and Michael took them home to read and to search for the patterns and trends that would emerge over several weeks and months of collecting employee and customer concerns and suggestions. On Friday morning, he'd call everyone together for what became known as "the hour of horror." Employees would gather around and brainstorm solutions to some—but not all—of the problems.

Being selective was smart because Michael Dell understood the concept of compound interest. He knew then, as my savviest clients do today, that if you solve just one percent of your problems or make a one percent improvement in your products and services each week, you'll gain greater and greater yields from the solutions with each passing year. If, on the other hand, you aim for solving too many problems, you'll have made a hassle out of your de-hassling system! Instead of being your key productivity-enhancing tool, it'll become just another drag on everybody's time.

Gathering the Data:
Be Encouraging, Be Responsive

To get started, ask your customers and employees a three-part question: What should we start doing, what should we stop doing, and what should we continue doing? For employees, have them think about these questions from both their perspective and the perspective of customers. This initial survey will let people get things off their chests, especially if they haven't had the chance before. Compile the data, call a meeting, and brainstorm some solutions. Don't make it a chore; make it fun. Then, in your company newsletter or weekly CEO communication, report progress on some of the stickier, long-term issues that have cropped up. That'll pave the way for introducing a more systematic ongoing process for collecting this feedback using a manual or electronic logging process. This ongoing process encourages and requires your employees to log recurring problems they and your customers are experiencing. Suggest that you want to hear about anything and everything that caused them to spend more than a minute doing something that shouldn't have needed doing. What are customers requesting that can't be provided? Where are they being hassled in the process of doing business with your firm? You might even prime the pump by holding a weekly prize drawing, and offer a raffle ticket for each hassle submitted until the habit becomes established. To make it clear this isn't a top-down directive, make your own executive-level list to share: What are the top 10 things that make *your* job a hassle?

The key is to get the raw, unedited data. Even if a problem occurred and was resolved, it needs to be logged so patterns and trends can be observed. At the Ritz Carlton hotels, noted for winning two Malcolm Baldrige awards for outstanding quality and service, personnel are required to log all incidences of customer or employee problems or concerns and turn them in daily to the general manager. This data points out opportunities for improvement that save time, improve working conditions, and increase customer delight.

Handling the Feedback

The trick to getting your de-hassling system humming is to be responsive. If employees feel their feedback is dropping into a black hole, it'll dry up. Initially, find some quick-hit solutions. If there needs to be a bigger wastebasket in the women's restroom, get a new one in there pronto. If there are bigger, thornier issues (I find they're usually related to IT or billing), put a team on one or two of them and schedule regular updates.

There's no way to predict how much hassle input you'll receive. You could get a lot; you could get a little. If your team is reluctant to provide feedback, don't shame them; just work extra hard to respond to the few items you receive. You'll get more participants next time, I promise. If, on the other hand, you find yourself swamped with input, don't give in to the temptation to omit items, combine them, or summarize them. Get the raw data out there even if the initial list numbers 1,784 items, as it did the first time I did this with a client over a decade ago. People are watching to see if their contributions are being considered. Again, don't summarize the data, give it back to the team in raw form. The only exception is if the feedback includes personal attacks. These should be dealt with privately.

Some companies handle long lists by posting them on a website or sending them out via e-mail. In Boston, a company called The Mathworks has established an internal online interest group where people can log and discuss their hassles. I've seen a few companies ask their employees to categorize their beefs by checking topic boxes but remember, nobody should feel they've been summarized away.

Reporting Progress

People will want to see change as it's occurring. At Columbia University Business School some years ago, the dean posted a bulletin board for complaints and suggestions. Students and faculty alike knew they'd been heard when he scrawled on the notecards "Noted, done." Closing the loop in this fashion is absolutely crucial. Let people know what issues are being addressed, and which ones have been resolved. If it's something you can't do anything about, say more than that—*lots* more. When a customer bemoans the loss of a product at Sundance, a locally owned natural food store in Eugene, Oregon, leadership may devote a page to explaining the vicissitudes of dealing with distribution companies—and they'll post it for all to see, right next to the original complaint. People may not be pleased, but at least now they understand.

Some companies will even keep an issues-aging report, tracking how long an issue has been outstanding, so it doesn't fall through the cracks. McVantage had a simple way to keep the issues "in sight, in mind." They wrote each issue on a large roll of paper and posted it on the factory wall where it stayed until it was resolved.

De-Hassling Etiquette 101

Now that we've sketched out a customer and employee feedback system in broad strokes, let's spend a little time on the finer points. In the wrong hands, a de-hassling system can become an elaborate waste of time, or worse yet, a newfangled version of the old-fashioned corporate witch hunt. Don't let it happen to you. Use my six-point set of problem-solving guidelines (found at the end of the chapter) weekly, monthly, whenever—just to keep you on track.

The first three of my six guidelines have to do with getting your hassles under a microscope, checking them for relevancy and specificity, then making sure you're addressing the root of the issue. Why tackle one particular hassle if there are others that have greater impact on how your company works (relevancy)? Go after what's causing the most pain in the organization. Why gallop off to solve "communications problems" if you're not sure whether somebody's talking about facts or fiction (specificity)? Don't let people get away with saying "the system's always down." Find out when, where and what are the patterns. And are you sure you're not treating the symptoms instead of curing the disease (address the root)?

I remember surveying employees for a client in Tennessee. The number one issue was that "all the customers are mad" which was leading to the customers abusing the associates. Clearly this was a relevant issue. However, the use of the term "all" pointed out a need to get specifics. Looking further into the issues, we found that the warehouse was mis-shipping various items. We then turned to looking for the root of the problem. A key technique is asking "Why" several times. Why were items being mis-shipped? We discovered that the fifth copy of a five-part form was difficult to read. So why was it hard to read? Because the impact printer spitting out these picking forms had a worn-out impact print wheel (most of you won't know what this is!). The point: many big problems trace back to simple solutions if you'll just get detective Colombo-like and ask a lot of questions. And along the way, someone might ask why the system needs five copies in the first place!

The remaining three guidelines on my six-point list have to do with keeping your de-hassling system fair and humane: focus on the process (the "what") and not the people (the "who"): involve all those affected; never backstab.

To avoid having the feedback degenerate into name-calling, focus on the what, not the who. When all the what's keep leading to the same who, of course, you may need to free up that person's future. And in that case, you still need to identify the "what" behind the failure of the "who" or you're destined to make the same hiring mistake. But that's rare. Most hassles are process hassles, not people hassles.

To save you the chore of running around to ten people and hearing ten different stories, be sure to involve all those affected. One of our major aircraft manufacturers found it could save a half-million dollars per jet, just by getting the whole team together to discuss problems instead of talking in smaller groups.

Finally, never backstab. We all have the right to face our accuser. Besides, we're more likely to get to the root of the problem when all those affected are in the same room and thus less likely to attack the "who."

With these guidelines in place, you'll ensure that your customer and employee-feedback system raises morale instead of defeating it, and improves productivity, rather than sapping it.

Leadership-Development Opportunities

Surely by now you've thought, "Great, an employee feedback system. Another task to add to my already-bulging job description." But de-hassling your organization doesn't have to fall on the backs of the executive team. In fact, it's better to form a mid-level leadership team to handle the initial screening and problem solving. Who else is as close to the action? Not you. Who better to know which items deserve priority attention and which employees are best suited to finding the solution? Again, probably not you. Think of it as a leadership-development opportunity, an investment in your eventual succession plan, as your supervisors and mid-level leaders have the opportunity to creatively address issues and improve performance and customer satisfaction.

Taking it one step further, Zingerman's Deli has the best change management process I've found. If any employee sees a problem, they launch an improvement project using a four step process.

As an example, one of Zingerman's employees felt the mailbox needed moved closer to the entrance of their warehouse.

Step 1: write a two or three paragraph (not pages) envisioned future—how will everyone be better off with this change, including how people will feel.

Step 2: make a list of all the people who need to sign off on the project. This would include the person who has a move the mailbox, the CFO having to approve the expenditure, and the person delivering the mail.

Step 3: visit each and share the envisioned future. If 100% buy-in is achieved, then

Step 4: initiate the change as the project lead.

This process empowers Zingerman's over 700 full and part time employees to actively and continuously improve every aspect of the organization in an organized way. And through this process employees come to learn the cross-functional nature of almost all decisions and meet people throughout the organization.

Daily and Weekly Measures

The following sections will help you define what daily and weekly measures you and your company should focus on to drive performance, guide priorities, and help anticipate problems and opportunities. These measures will also help everyone in the company answer the fundamental question, "Did I have a good day or week?" which provides an objective indication of progress important to maintaining morale and enthusiasm.

Critical Numbers

It's best if the company has one Critical Number around which to align the company over the next quarter or year. A Critical Number represents a key short-term focus in the company that will have the most impact on the future of the firm. For instance, Dell Computer chose increasing the ratio of server sales to PC sales as their focus for 2001, knowing that this would focus the organization on transitioning from the PC market, which was slowing down in growth, to the fastergrowth server market. Overall, the key question to ask is "What is the single most important measurable thing we need to accomplish in the next 3 to 12 months?" And I want to emphasize that this focus should change regularly to improve different aspects of the organization. It's like a weightlifter who focuses on different muscle groups during each workout to maintain proper proportions and to keep it interesting. It also lets different muscle groups rest.

Moneyball Stats

Next, the executive team should identify one to three Moneyball stats that give them insight into how the company is likely to do in the future. The ability to predict is a key leadership function. The term "Moneyball" comes from the book and movie by the same name. Using data analytics, Oakland A's general manager Billy Beane found statistics that better predicted success than the standard measures baseball had used for over a century to select and compensate players. Beane's successful approach using data analytics now permeates every sport on the planet.

A Moneyball stat is typically a complex ratio, like the quarterback efficiency ratio in American football, made up of key indicators like the ratio of sales this week against the same week last year compared to the growth rate of the market. This would tell you if you're really gaining market share or not. Or you might look at the ratio of sales calls made to those closed to give an indication of sales effectiveness. One CEO I met simply counted the number of trucks at the loading dock compared to the number of orders that week to know if it was going to be a good month next month. These key weekly measures make you smarter about how the business is doing. Once you've discovered the right Moneyball stats, you need to stick with them for a period of time to see if they continue to correlate to success.

Measures for Everyone

Once the Moneyball stats and Critical Number are decided, every person or team should have one or two daily or weekly measures that align with these numbers. The key is *alignment* or what Jack Stack, author of the *Great Game of Business*, calls "line of sight." Can every employee see how what they're doing impacts the entire firm? One organization chose improving their customer service rating as a Critical Number to focus on for one quarter. Based on this, every employee or team figured out something they could do better to improve this rating, from improving the speed of response, to accuracy of ordertaking, to timeliness of returning phone calls.

Highly Visible

Make your measurements visible. Like the huge scoreboards at sporting events, your company-wide measurements—preferably in some graphical form—should be on large charts or television screens placed where the individual, team, or company can see the results. And I strongly suggest that every office employee have some kind of whiteboard in their cubicle or office on which to graph their own daily and weekly measures. These numbers have a much greater impact if people see them on a large graph. It is even better if they have to plot the numbers themselves. There's something powerful in having to physically plot the points and connect the dots on the graph to bring the results alive and make them personal. It's also useful to display last year's results on the graph along with a projected or budgeted target line.

Prediction

Once the habit of daily and weekly measuring is established, you want to start projecting ahead in addition to simply documenting the past. Jack Stack calls this Forward Forecasting. This involves making an educated guess about how the next few weeks or months are likely to turn out based on what you know now. Then, by comparing actual results against predicted results, you'll begin to learn how to better predict outcomes and strengthen your knowledge about what drives results for yourself, your team, and the company.

Situation Room

I recommend creating a situation room for the executive team. A situation room is where you display your core values and purpose, priorities for the quarter and year, and a map of the geographical territory you cover. Also display your Moneyball stats and Critical Number large and graphically. Make someone accountable for making sure the displays are up-to-date.

If you do not have a separate room and you don't want visitors seeing your information, get an easel on wheels for about $300 that has a whiteboard on one side and a corkboard on the other. Use the white-board for general discussions and then, for your weekly executive team meeting, turn it around to show the corkboard side, where you have mounted all your maps, graphs, and lists. There are also reversible whiteboards that hang on the wall, or you can place the information behind a curtain along one end of the room. However, many firms proudly display this information even for customers to see, giving customers confidence that the firm is well managed and the executive team well informed.

Summary

In summary, it is absolutely essential that you develop daily and weekly measurements for the company, and daily and weekly measurements for every individual or team that align with the company measures. These numbers focus everyone's attention on driving performance, reinforcing priorities, and helping anticipate problems and opportunities. Make these measurements highly visible and graphical for everyone to see and create a situation room for the executive team. Most importantly, just start measuring something and keep tracking different metrics until you find those that provide the most insight and useful feedback.

Problem-Solving Guidelines

You might note that these guidelines are similar to those found in conflict-resolution, decision-making, and problem-solving courses.

Relevancy—Does the issue really matter, is it of top importance, is there a customer affected by the hassle? Here you are looking for a pattern of recurring hassles. You can't solve every hassle right away, so you want to look at those that are costing customers and employees the most time or money.

Be Specific—Look back over your hassle lists. Did you write in generalities or list specifics? Some people will list as a hassle, communications problems, or interruptions, or having to answer the same questions over and over. However, you can't begin to address these issues without knowing the who, what, when, where, how, and why of these hassles. Being specific also means being careful when using the words "always," "never," and "all the time." In staff meetings, push people to give specifics.

Address the Root—Look at the cause of the issue and not just the symptoms. Let's say you've identified a specific communications problem—in most cases, the standard response is "send out a memo." Rarely does this get to the root of the problem—instead, it serves as a quick fix. One of the best ways to get to the root of the problem is using the "5 Whys" technique. Ask "why" several times until you get to the root cause.

Focus on the What, Not the Who—You don't want to turn your search into a finger-pointing or blame game. Besides, 95 percent of the time, it's a process problem, not a people problem. However, if all the what's keep leading to the same who, maybe you've waited too long and the person has to be let go. But you should still ask "What did we do wrong that caused this person to fail?" Maybe your hiring or training process needs to be improved. If you don't get to the root of the *what*, you'll keep making the same who mistakes.

Involve All Those Affected—Rather than run around getting ten explanations from ten people, get them all in the same room to give a truer picture of the entire problem. Getting everyone in the room together also helps to minimize suboptimization—where fixing a problem in one part of the organization causes greater problems elsewhere.

Never Backstab—Never talk negatively about anyone if that person is not present. The only exception is if you need to seek the advice of someone before confronting the individual. In this case, you still need to bring the individual into the conversation as soon as possible. This guideline has its roots in such principles as the right to face your accuser and to be present when being judged. Besides, when you talk negatively about someone to another person, they then wonder if you are talking negatively about them behind their back. If you can be successful in implementing this rule, the level of trust and openness in your organization will improve immensely. And when the other person is present, everyone tends to follow the first five guidelines more closely.

5

BRAND PROMISE

*The single most important deliverable
in building company value!*

Executive Summary: What really matters to your customers? What is the #1 job the customer needs you to do for them? What is it that brings your customers to you, and keeps those customers loyally returning, purchase after purchase, year after year? It's your brand promise— the key factor that sets you apart from all competitors. Your brand promise is the starting point from which all other executive decisions are derived. In this chapter, you'll gain valuable tips that will assist you in identifying a brand promise that is both competitive and measurable. Through real-life examples, you'll also see how successful companies evolve and change their brand promise over time. Finally, you'll obtain a tool at the end of this chapter to guide you in determining the brand promise most suited to your strategy.

Think back to when Federal Express burst on the scene in the early eighties. What was it that made Fred Smith's new company such a sensation? The answer: It got packages where they were going overnight, no ifs, ands, or buts—"absolutely, positively" on time. Send your package via FedEx and you knew your recipient will be holding it by 10:00 a.m. That was Federal Express's come-on to a world that previously knew only the postal service. It was FedEx's measurable brand promise.

FedEx's 10:00 a.m. deadline was more than a marketing slogan. It was the key decision that drove all others. To make the promised arrival on time, FedEx knows it needs to get its planes out of Memphis by 2:00 a.m. To get the planes in the air on time, FedEx needs me to get my package to the station at Dulles Airport by 10:00 pm. Backing up even further on the timeline, the FedEx box nearest my home has a 5:15 p.m. pickup time to allow the orange-and-purple truck to complete its route and get to the airport. From the first business plan Smith wrote, and up until quite recently, the company's strategies and tactics existed simply to deliver on this one measurable brand promise. (Nowadays, Smith's delivering on a somewhat different brand promise. More on that later.)

Determining a brand promise is the #1 strategy decision for any company. Choose the right one—the one your customers respond to, the one you can track and execute day after day—and you win. It's that simple. Choose the wrong one and you'll probably flounder for years, never hitting your goals. So how do you choose the right brand promise for your organization?

Start by taking four minutes to watch Clay Christensen's "Job of a Milkshake" video. Christensen popularized the key strategy question "what is the job to be done by your product or service?"

In the mini case study, Christensen shares how McDonald's was trying to increase the sales of their milkshakes. They had tried everything —chocolater, chewier—but nothing worked until they gathered first hand data by standing outside a restaurant and seeing who and why they were purchasing milkshakes.

McDonald's found they had various groups of customers—buyer personas—purchasing milkshakes to do different jobs for them. There is the lone morning commuter who needs the milkshake to entertain them while on a long boring commute. Having a tiny straw to increase the time it takes to consume the milkshake, and nothing chunky to clog up the straw are two key aspects of that milkshake experience. In the afternoon, a different group of buyers were parents needing to entertain and distract their children without ruining dinner. In short, McDonald's isn't in the job of making milkshakes; they have different jobs to do for different groups of customers.

Scaling Up has a client with private MBA schools in India. When the owner realized his #1 job to do for his students is to help them get the right first job that propels their career, it changed the nature of their 100% offering and propelled them past their competition.

FedEx's #1 job is to get the package to the recipient on-time. The #1 job of Google is search. The #1 job of Volvo is to get you from point A to B (which all cars should do) the safest. This is what we refer to as the #1 measurable brand promise.

NOTE: For more on the importance of having and communicating a measurable brand promise, in order to drive valuation, please read the 2024 HBR article "The Right Way to Build Your Brand."

Define Your Sandbox

Next, figure out your desired sphere of influence over the next three-to-five years. Are you destined to remain a local company, with customers in one or two cities? Or will you grow to be regional, national, maybe even international? This may not be as obvious a decision as it sounds. And don't assume you can't be a local company and still have some pretty high aspirations, because you can.

When you're done defining your sandbox geographically, take some time to think about your customers and their demographics. Who will you be selling to over the next three to five years? Are there some customers you'll choose to leave to somebody else? Will it take any special techniques to reach your desired customers?

Lastly, consider how many product lines you can logically and reasonably carry. Don't forget to figure out which distribution channels make the most sense for your enterprise. Logistical considerations can make or break your long-range goals. Scaling Up's sandbox is delivering coaching, training, and performance platform globally to firms with revenues between $5 million and $500 million, aiming to grow at least 20 percent per year. We utilize a direct-sales model and deliver services through over 250 coaching partners on six continents.

Determine Customer Needs

Based on the sandbox you've defined, ask yourself: what is your customers' greatest need—job to be done by your product or service? I'm not asking about their wants—they'll "want, want, want" you all the way to bankruptcy if you let them! What you're looking for is what really matters to the customer. At the same time, you want it to be something that demonstrably differentiates you from the competition.

By way of example, consider the commercial furniture business. If you've bought a suite of office furniture, you can attest that it's often difficult to tell the difference between one company's brand and those of their three top competitors. So, what's the fundamental need of the customer? If you consider the customer to be the facilities manager who's making the furniture purchase, the #1 need is to not get yelled at by the CEO and the rest of the executive team. Nobody's going to yell over issues of quality or style. No, what's going to make the executive team read the riot act is a missing part or an installation issue. And, believe it, the manager has enough friends in facility management to know which furniture company falls short on these key details. The facility manager is going to go with the company that says, in essence, "we'll protect your reputation as a facility manager."

Determining customer needs is a tougher task when you've got two sets of customers, as does job search firm Orion International. But, when CEO Jim Tully began working out his company's measurable brand promise, he realized that speed was attractive to both the job candidates Orion deals with and the corporate clients that are Orion's bread and butter. Job candidates want to know that searches and hiring will be completed quickly, and HR professionals want to rely on Orion to fill their vacancies ASAP. Ideally, Tully needed to find a single brand promise to please both sets of customers, while differentiating himself from his competition. Speed seemed key.

What's Your Measurable Brand Promise?

For Jim Tully at Orion International, the measurable brand promise he hit upon is what he calls "14 Days Done"—whereby Orion will complete a hiring process in two weeks flat if the client requests it. No other competitor makes such a promise, so it's a potent differentiator in the marketplace. What's more, it's a financially beneficial strategy, because a process that used to take an average of 60 days to complete and be billed now averages 26 days. This shortened cycle time has resulted in better cash flow. It also increased revenues by 78.5 percent within months of implementing "14 Days Done."

However, Tully's brand promise is not only measurable at the end of the placement process. He and his executives quickly realized that their key measurable comes somewhat earlier, in the number of final interviews conducted. That tally gives them a fair guess at how they'll end the month. And they didn't stop measuring there. Tully's team went back over the entire placement cycle, considering each step in the process as a potential moneymaker. They realized that "every step of the way, everything has some value," as Tully puts it.

For a different kind of measurable brand promise, look to Boston Beer, makers of Sam Adams beer. Founder James Koch comes from several generations of brew masters, and his aim and differentiator in the market has always been to make a better-tasting beer—the best, in fact. How does he make that both believable and measurable? By winning major beer competitions. Sam Adams won a consumer-preference poll four years in a row—until the poll was discontinued with that fourth win in 1989. Since then, Sam Adams has competed extraordinarily well in blind taste tests based on style, held at the annual Great American Beer Festival. In 1997, the beer won an unprecedented three gold medals there. What's more, Sam Adams beers have won at least one top honor at the GABF for fourteen consecutive years. That gives Boston Beer Company more medal-winning beers than any other craft brewer. Clearly, Boston Beer has earned the right to market its products (of which Sam Adams is but one) as The World's Most Award-Winning Beers.

Bear in mind: your brand promise shouldn't be easily accomplished. It ought to cause some stress in your organization to achieve. For a lofty brand promise example, look to Intuit, makers of the Quicken bookkeeping software for individuals and small businesses. Intuit's initial brand promise was ease of use. To back it up and make it measurable, Intuit promised unlimited support on a $59 piece of software. Clearly, that caused some heart palpitations among designers and managers alike, but it brought out the best in the organization. That unlimited-support promise drove every decision in the company—from how to build the product to how to communicate with customers—so that the customer wouldn't have to call. And it gave Quicken the solid foothold it needed to get established and grow. Today, it garners over 80 percent market share of the small business accounting software niche.

If there is but one warning I can offer you as you hone in on your own measurable brand promise, it's to avoid getting caught up in marketing slogans. This is often a point of confusion when seeking a brand promise. Don't get caught up in the wording of a slogan and forget the essence of the exercise. Stay pure. Find the measurable deliverable and leave the sloganeering to the marketing folks. Fred Smith's key decision at FedEx was the promised arrival time. It was up to the marketing firm to convert that advantage into a marketing message.

Control Your Bottleneck or Chokepoint

Now that you've put a stake in the ground by determining your measurable brand promise, what are you going to do to lock it up, to hold that position? How will you build a mote around your business making it difficult for competitors to compete?

You start by looking for the bottlenecks or chokepoints in your industry—there's always one or two—and figure out a strategy to either blow them up or neutralize their threat. For instance, early in the oil business John D. Rockefeller determined that the real shortage in the industry was not oil (it was gushing out of the ground) or refineries (over 1,000 popped up overnight), but oak barrels for capturing the oil, and very specifically, the iron rings that hold the oak slats together. So, one of his first acquisitions was a key firm that made the all-important iron rings. Later, when it became clear that transportation costs were the biggest threat to profitability, Rockefeller shifted his energies to that chokepoint.

Let's go back to Intuit and consider Quicken's chokepoint. If you've used bookkeeping software for a while, you know that, in the beginning, one of the trickiest elements of bill paying was lining up the pre-printed paper checks in the printer (back when those were popular). That's true because every printer is—or at least was—a little different. Intuit eventually controlled this bottleneck or chokepoint by having the Quicken standard built into every printer made. Such foresightedness gave Quicken a huge advantage in its burgeoning market. It controlled the chokepoint.

At Boston Beer, founder Koch believes the chokepoint is his hops supply. In fact, he has said that he attributes the honors his beers have won in major competitions to the very select hops he purchases from a special few acres in Bavaria. Not surprisingly, one of the world's largest beer manufacturers once attempted to purchase that acreage, thus locking up the world's supply of these special hops. Luckily, Koch got wind of the attempted purchase, and reasserted his right to them in the nick of time. That, too, is a fine example of controlling your chokepoint.

Everything Changes—
Including Your Brand Promise

Federal Express isn't touting delivery at 10:00 a.m. as a brand promise anymore. Why? Because things change and that includes brand promises.

Federal Express lost its brand promise due to its own success. Today, there are many shippers making overnight delivery claims, even the U.S. Postal Service. Delivery by 10:00 a.m. is now merely table stakes. You can't even be a player in the shipping business unless you can perform on that once-revolutionary brand promise of overnight delivery.

FedEx's latest brand promise takes it to the next level, which is "peace of mind." The measurable deliverable is the customer's ability to know where his or her package is at all times. What customers want today is tracking. FedEx figured that out several years ago, and quietly spent roughly a billion dollars making sure that customers, big and small, had the necessary terminals installed to handle this new tracking capability. They handed out disks containing the necessary software like so many AOL freebies. Now the brand promise is being sold via the marketing slogan, "Be absolutely sure," and you've probably seen the commercial in which the crocodile hunter keels over from snakebite. Cheerful to the end, the croc hunter acknowledges that the anti-venom was shipped through another carrier, "not Federal Express." Then his eyes roll back in his head and he collapses off-camera.

Please note that Federal Express hasn't stopped guaranteeing delivery at 10:00 a.m.; they've just upped the ante. They deliver early and their tracking gives you peace of mind. In a couple of years, it'll probably be early delivery and tracking and...well, something else, as the previous brand promise becomes mere table stakes. Just like Federal Express's, your once-revolutionary brand promise will someday become table stakes, and probably sooner rather than later. Start working now on the next value-added improvement. If you don't, somebody else will beat you to it.

Your measurable brand promise is crucial. It defines your company in the minds of the public. It gives your organization something huge and galvanizing to strive toward. It does not overstate it one whit to say that your brand promise is a single-minded measure around which all strategic and tactical decisions are made. By considering your BHAG, defining your sandbox, determining customer needs, and controlling your bottleneck or chokepoint, you'll have a measurable brand promise that will set you apart from your competition. That is, until your competition catches up and forces you to up the ante with a new and equally inspiring brand promise.

Jim Collins' Flywheel

As noted in the beginning of this chapter, everything starts with identifying your #1 brand promise—job to be done. The same for the Flywheel effect Jim Collins describes in his book *Good to Great* and monograph entitled *Turning the Flywheel*. The latter is a quick read and important for all business leaders to read. The starting point of all flywheels is the firm's #1 brand promise.

In the case of Vanguard, featured in one of Collins' examples, it's "offer lower cost mutual funds." Southwest Airlines starts with something similar "low fare."

Brand Promise from Customer Perspective

Last, it's critical your firm sets and measures the brand promise from the customers' perspective. When Southwest Airlines promised low airfare, it was set to be less than bus fare, not just lower than other competing airlines.

When McDonald's promises "fast" it's measured from when someone first considers wanting something to eat to when they are back doing what they were doing. This is more comprehensive than simply filling an order quickly. Wendy's was our preferred fast food chain with a faster drive through, yet it was 20 minutes from our home. McDonald's had two restaurants with 4 minutes depending on which route we were taking.

Deciding who you want to serve—buyer personas—and what is each of their measured "job to be done" is THE critical strategy question that powers the rest of your business strategy and execution.

For our firm Scaling Up, our buyer persona is an organizational leader who wants to scale any size firm—from startups to scaleups to unicorns. And our brand promise is to provide a 100% solution of coaching, training, and technology platforms to "scale valuation."

Every decision you and your team makes should be measured against whether it will increase or decrease the value (valuation) of your growing firm. We can help guide you in this process.

Value-Add

Who is your main customer(s)—buyer persona(s)?

How do you define your Sandbox—geography, product lines, distribution channels?

What is the biggest "need"—job to be done—your customers have, distinguished from all their "wants"?

What is your measurable Brand Promise?

What is the bottleneck/shortage/chokepoint in your sandbox/industry and how are you going to control it?

What are you going to do to utilize technology to maintain control of the chokepoint/constraint?

6

ONE-PAGE STRATEGIC PLAN

Keeping it simple keeps it clear!

Executive summary: The bigger your company gets, and the faster it's growing, the harder it is to get everybody on the same page. The problem, of course, is that there isn't a single page around which to align. Instead, there are likely more than a dozen pages, actual and imaginary, along with memos and e-mails, each purporting to describe your company's vision, mission, and strategy. Further, many of these messages may be riddled with unclear and even contradictory statements about who your company is, what it does, and how. This chapter will introduce you to the Vision Summary, SWT, and One-Page Strategic Plan, simple yet powerful one-page tools that help you edit your vision and strategy down to a single, action-oriented page. Go to *www.ScalingUp.com* to download our free one-page Growth Tools™ in multiple languages.

Back when your company was just getting started, and you were struggling to get the job done with three or four key people, confusion over the vision was unheard of. Everybody was eating and sleeping the company's goals, just as you were. Your employees knew as well as you did which task was critical because they all were! Rarely did people complain about communication problems.

But with each new level of growth, and each new hire, your influence over the organization necessarily grows more arm's-length. You begin to delegate low-level strategic decisions, and not surprisingly, some of the calls your associates make leave you scratching your head. Perhaps misunderstandings have cropped up between associates, each side believing they were doing what they were supposed to. Maybe customers are complaining about mistakes, or—worse— neglect. The ugly truth is plain: the vision and strategy that always seemed so clear to you, as the entrepreneurial brains of the company, have gotten muddled somewhere along the way. Where once you could relay an idea to a handful of close associates and have it understood and implemented immediately, you now find it takes days or weeks to get the concept out laterally. Then it might take more weeks, even months, to communicate the information to the lowest levels of the organization. And when you're done, people will still clamor for more and better communication.

If you're thinking, "Yes, but that's just how it is when companies get bigger," you should know that there are tools for handling the increasing complexity business growth generates. Maybe there was a time when companies could rationalize their poor internal communication as just the unfortunate by-product of success. Maybe they could get by from year to year, just resting on the laurels of a respected name and a commanding market share. If so, those days are long gone. Thanks to global competition, the rise of e-commerce and the ever-quickening pace of innovation, clear communication of an effective strategy is absolutely essential to survival. To become and remain competitive, your organization needs three things:

1. a **framework** that identifies and supports your corporate strategy,
2. a common **language** in which to express that strategy, and,
3. a well-developed **habit** of using this framework and language to continually evaluate your strategic progress.

Most important, you've got to keep it simple. Who has time to read— let alone develop—packets and pamphlets of forgettable prose? You've got to boil your expression of strategic might down to one powerful, useable, post-able, and thoroughly unforgettable page.

Meet the strategic framework that works best for emerging companies. It's called the Planning Pyramid *(Figure 6-1)*. As consultants to growing companies of all stripes and types for more than forty-years, we've seen what works in establishing an effective vision and have incorporated these best practices into a concise tool. The pyramid graphically conveys to everyone in your organization how the various vision

Figure 6-1

The Planning Pyramid:
A Strategic Framework

Accountability

DAILY →		← WHO
WEEKLY →	Schedule	← WHEN
QUARTERLY →	Actions	HOW
ANNUALLY →	Goals	WHAT
3–5 YRS. →	Targets	WHERE
LIFE of LEADER →	Purpose	WHY
FOREVER →	Core Values	SHOULD

TIME FRAME

1% Vision, 99% Alignment

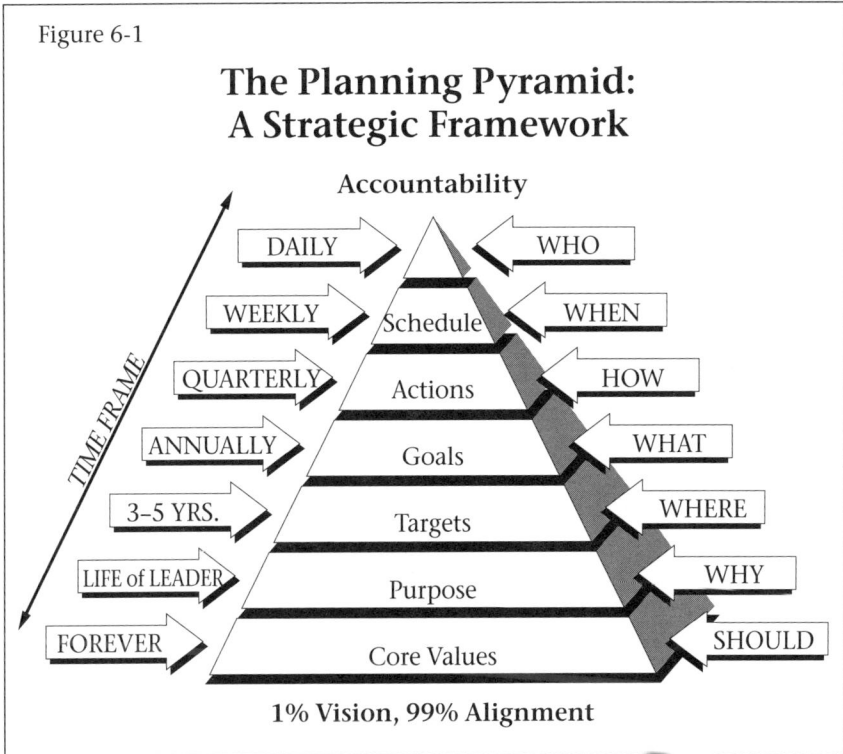

pieces—values, purpose, targets, goals, actions, schedules and accountabilities—align, establishing a common strategic language that is easy to use and helps eliminate confusion. The One-Page Strategic Plan (OPSP) *(Figure 6-2)* provides the tool for getting it all down on paper.

From the ScalingUp.com website, you may download an editable PDF document or print it out and fill it in by hand. When you print it out, place the 1st page to the left of the 2nd page, giving you a continuous, single-page document on an 11-by-17-inch piece of paper.

If you don't want to do this right now, read through the rest of this chapter to give you a sense of the language and process I suggest for defining a whole vision. A vision is a dream with a plan. Without all seven levels of the Planning Pyramid delineated, your vision will be less than complete.

The One-Page Strategic Plan is essentially the Planning Pyramid turned on its side. The tool aligns both horizontally and vertically, providing a logical framework for organizing your strategic vision and

Strategy: One-Page Strategic Plan (OPSP)   Organization Name:

People (Reputation Drivers)

Employees	Customers	Shareholders
1. _____	1. _____	1. _____
2. _____	2. _____	2. _____
3. _____	3. _____	3. _____

CORE VALUES/BELIEFS (Should/Shouldn't)	PURPOSE (Why)	TARGETS (3–5 YRS.) (Where)	GOALS (1 YR.) (What)

TARGETS (3–5 YRS.)

Future Date	
Revenues	
Profit	
Mkt. Cap/Cash	

Sandbox

GOALS (1 YR.)

Yr Ending	
Revenues	
Profit	
Mkt. Cap	
Gross Margin	
Cash	
A/R Days	
Inv. Days	
Rev./Emp.	

Actions To Live Values, Purposes, BHAG	*Key Thrusts/Capabilities* 3-5 Year Priorities	*Key Initiatives* 1 Year Priorities
1	1	1
2	2	2
3	3	3
4	4	4
5	5	5

Profit per X	**Brand Promise KPIs**	**Critical #: People or B/S**
		■
		▨
		▨ *Between green & red*
		■

BHAG®	**Brand Promises**	**Critical #: Process or P/L**
		■
		▨
		▨ *Between green & red*
		■

Strengths/Core Competencies

1. _____
2. _____
3. _____

Weaknesses:

1. _____
2. _____
3. _____

BHAG is a Registered Trademark of Jim Collins and Jerry Porras.

SCALING UP
A GAZELLES COMPANY

Your Name: _____   Date: _____

Process (Productivity Drivers)

Make/Buy	Sell	Recordkeeping
1. _____	1. _____	1. _____
2. _____	2. _____	2. _____
3. _____	3. _____	3. _____

ACTIONS (QTR) (How)	THEME (QTR/ANNUAL)	YOUR ACCOUNTABILITY (Who/When)

ACTIONS (QTR)

Qtr #	
Revenues	
Profit	
Mkt. Cap	
Gross Margin	
Cash	
A/R Days	
Inv. Days	
Rev./Emp.	

THEME

Deadline:	
Measurable Target/Critical #	

Theme Name

YOUR ACCOUNTABILITY

	Your KPIs	Goal
1		
2		
3		

Rocks

	Quarterly Priorities	Who
1		
2		
3		
4		
5		

Scoreboard Design

Describe and/or sketch your design in this space

	Your Quarterly Priorities	Due
1		
2		
3		
4		
5		

Critical #: People or B/S
- ■
- ■
- ▨ *Between green & red*
- ■

Celebration

Critical #: People or B/S
- ■
- ■
- ▨ *Between green & red*
- ■

Critical #: Process or P/L
- ■
- ■
- ▨ *Between green & red*
- ■

Reward

Critical #: Process or P/L
- ■
- ■
- ▨ *Between green & red*
- ■

Trends

1. _____	4. _____
2. _____	5. _____
3. _____	6. _____

BHAG is a Registered Trademark of Jim Collins and Jerry Porras.

guaranteeing that you have all the pieces to make it whole. The physical structure of the tool forces prioritization, which is key.

No organization or individual can focus on or accomplish more than three to five priorities in a given time period. The One-Page Strategic Plan forces you to select what I call your Top 5 and Top 1 of 5 priorities.

But first, I want to introduce a simplified version of the OPSP: the Vision Summary.

Many companies can start with this, including startups, and then progress to the more comprehensive OPSP as their sophistication in strategic planning increases.

Vision Summary

The Vision Summary provides a simplified OPSP framework for companies just getting started with implementing Scaling Up and for firms with 50 employees or fewer. For larger firms that are taking advantage of the more detailed aspects of the OPSP, the Vision Summary provides a one-page format to communicate key aspects of the company's vision to employees, customers, investors, and the broader community.

At *scalingup.com*, you can download a copy of the Vision Summary without the Scaling Up logo in the upper right. Then list the following for your company:

- Core Values
- Purpose
- Brand Promises
- Big Hairy Audacious Goal (BHAG®)

They represent the key components of the company's vision that every employee should know and understand thoroughly, making this summary useful as a key onboarding tool for new employees as well.

Under these components is a place to list the strategic priorities. In the first column, list the three- to five-year Key Thrusts/Capabilities from the OPSP. These are the handful of major medium-term priorities, which we will describe in more detail later.

In the middle column, list the year's #1 Priority and the Key Initiatives necessary to achieve it. And in the last column, list the quarter's #1 Priority and the "Rocks" required to reach this goal. We will provide more detail on how to set these priorities in "Mastering the Quarterly Theme" chapter.

These strategic components and priorities provide a quick snapshot of the company's vision. Underneath them is a place for every employee or team to personalize the plan. There, they can list a handful of key performance indicators (KPIs), priorities, and a Critical Number for the quarter, which should support and align with the company's vision. These come from decisions made when completing the last column of the OPSP, and we detail them later in this chapter, as well.

We encourage team members to post this Vision Summary in their cubicles, their offices, or the cabs of their sanitation trucks as visual reminders of the organization's strategic plan and their part in making it a reality.

One-Page Strategic Plan (OPSP)

Many people have dreams. However, a vision is a dream with a plan: a One-Page Strategic Plan.

To flesh out the vision, you need to answer seven basic questions: *who, what, when, where, how, why*, and the often challenging question, "But *should* we or *shouldn't* we?" These questions anchor the seven columns of the OPSP. If you ever feel confused by the terminology that comes with strategic planning, always come back to these seven simple questions.

The terminology can be hard to follow. We are working to get our industry to align around a common language, agreeing on standard definitions of vision, purpose, values, priorities, etc. We are also using the OPSP to integrate the various visioning frameworks of thought leaders like Jim Collins, Gary Hamel, Jack Stack, and Stephen Covey, to name a few.

The tool is designed to align both horizontally and vertically, providing a logical framework to organize your strategic vision and guarantee that you have all the pieces to make it whole. The physical structure of the OPSP forces prioritization and simplicity. There's not a lot of space to write, so you must be concise.

As you fill in the document, think of it as a giant crossword or Sudoku puzzle. Figure out what you can, and let that help you determine the rest (e.g., Purpose and Brand Promise will triangulate back to the BHAG®). "Get it down; then get it right" is our mantra. A good plan now is better than a great plan too late.

There is one other important design element to the OPSP. Jim Collins discovered that enduring companies operate with a dual dynamic that he labeled "preserve the core/stimulate progress." This duality is built into the OPSP. The first three columns describe the core, which holds steady over time. The balance of the plan, as you move right, becomes more dynamic, stimulating progress to meet the trends, opportunities, and challenges of the marketplace.

NOTE: The OPSP is for internal consumption. It's designed to help a team get the technical aspects of the strategic plan correct vs. craft marketing messages (e.g., taglines). However, once you construct the plan, it will be faster and less costly, if you are using an outside marketing or ad agency, to create the external messaging to communicate your vision to employees, customers, and the broader community.

OPSP Experiences: Holganix, Markitforce, and Towne Park

Barrett Ersek, co-founder of natural-lawn-care firm Holganix in Pennsylvania, has created five companies over twenty-years, his first when he was 17-years-old. He describes the OPSP and other strategic habits of this methodology as a blueprint for what he needs to do to grow his business. "When I was in my 20s, I was running a business with a checkbook in my back pocket, and then for the first time in my life, someone gave me an instruction booklet," he says.

For Alan Higgins of Australia-based Markitforce, a point-of-sale and warehouse fulfillment firm, the OPSP is an "automatic decision-making machine." The founder and chief engagement officer notes: "If there's ever a fork in the road or a decision to be made, we refer back to the tool to see if we're on strategy. If we're not, we chat about whether we should walk away from the opportunity."

The OPSP is one of the most valuable tools at 15,000-employee Towne Park, a hospitality services firm based in Maryland, according to founder Jerry South. "It allows me to think strategically about the business and compartmentalizes some of the big decisions we are wrestling with and breaks them down to bite-sized pieces," South says. "Plus, it creates the clarity needed around what's important in the business."

Let's walk through the seven columns of the OPSP:

Column 1 (Should/Shouldn't): Lists a handful of rules defining the boundaries for decision-making —the *Shoulds* or *Shouldn'ts* represented by the Core Values.

Column 2 (Why): Expresses the impact the company wants to make in the world (or neighborhood), providing the meaning—the *Why*—behind everyone's efforts. It requires two main decisions:

- **Purpose** (often referred to as "mission"): the aspirational North Star or Southern Cross providing direction to the business
- **BHAG®** (**Big Hairy Audacious Goal**): the measurable piece of the Purpose that the business can achieve in the next 10 to 25 years

Column 3 (Where): Defines *Where* the company is headed in the next three to five years. Includes a description of the Sandbox in which the company wants to play (e.g., in terms of customers, geography, and product/service mix) and its measurable Brand Promises to those customers. It also summarizes a handful of major Capabilities and Key Thrusts the company must pursue.

Column 4 (What): Describes *What* results need to be achieved in the next 12 months. These are driven by a measurable #1 Priority (Critical Number) and a handful of "Rocks".

Column 5 (How): Details *How* the company plans to achieve its vision, focused on a measurable "next step" 90-day #1 Priority (Critical Number) and a handful of "Rocks."

Column 6 (Finish Lines and Fun): Describes the theme, celebration, and rewards associated with the #1 Priority for the quarter or year. The theme celebrations give everyone a definitive finish line and a chance to have some fun.

Column 7 (Who): Delineates *Who* is accountable for various aspects of the OPSP, detailing the KPIs, Rocks, and Critical Numbers for each employee or team.

Last, the *When* question is represented by each column's time frame.

Filling In the OPSP

Alignment and clarity start at the very top of the OPSP with the Organization Name. Organizations must align around a name that customers and employees (including the receptionist answering the phones) can remember and say. Finding that everyone called the company FedEx, Federal Express changed its name. Minnesota Mining and Manufacturing worked for a while, but the corporation is 3M today. HVLS Fan Company, whose large industrial fans were designed to be high-volume and low-speed, adopted the name Big Ass Fans after years of having customers use that moniker instead. Today, the business— recently renamed Big Ass Solutions—is one of the most widely recognized, fastest-growing companies in its niche. Other companies have exceedingly long and complex names that include generic terms like "Group" or "Inc." which no one ever uses. Consider dropping those extra words.

The "Organization Name" line can be used to signify whether the strategic vision applies only to a division or department within a firm. At JSJ, each of the six companies will list its respective name (e.g., "Sparks, a JSJ Business").

Finish the title area by adding your own name and the date. A few key points:

1. Some of you have names that are difficult to pronounce and spell. It might be best to simplify them, like many of our clients in Malaysia who go by their initials (hi, H.K. and C.K.!) or like my friend Nick Alexos, whose original name was Nicholas Alexopoulos. Or mimic performers and consider adopting a more memorable and business-friendly nickname (Gordon Sumner is known the world over as Sting).

2. To eliminate confusion over whether the month or day is listed first in the date, we suggest trying the global standard used by Cisco: the two-digit designation of the day, followed by the three-letter designation of the month, and then the four-digit designation of the year (e.g., 02 Feb 2022.)

We hate to be so picky, but alignment starts with getting agreement on the organization's name, your name, and the format of the date.

Strengths, Weaknesses, and Trends

Along the bottom of the OPSP is a place to summarize the company's top three inherent Strengths/Core Competencies and Weaknesses. There is also room to highlight the top six trends that will likely hit the company and its industry like meteors. These serve as the foundation upon which the Vision is built. Later in this chapter, we'll introduce a new one-page SWT tool to help you fill this in. It supplements the age-old SWOT that companies have used for decades.

OPSP Column 1: Core Values/Beliefs

Moving up to the body of the form, list the firm's Core Values in the first column. These three to eight phrases broadly define the shoulds and shouldn'ts that govern your company's underlying decisions and describe the personality of the organization. "Mastering the Core Values" chapter discusses in more detail Core Values and how to use them to drive the people (HR) systems inside your company.

NOTE: Do not feel compelled to call these concepts Core Values. Label them however you like: beliefs, rules, the HP Way. The key is to figure out what they are so your team can utilize them to keep the culture strong and drive decisions as the company scales.

OPSP Column 2:
Purpose, Profit per X, and BHAG®

If the first column represents the soul of the organization (or organism), then column 2 presents its heart. Column 2 answers some very basic *Why* questions: Why is this company doing what it's doing? What's its higher purpose? Why should I have passion for what we're doing?

It also provides a clue as to why certain seemingly small incidents send the founder into a tirade, while other situations, which may be bigger and more costly, slide by almost without comment. For example, Scaling Up's Purpose revolves around the word "contribution." We're excited to support the contribution scaleups make to their local and global economies and the contribution they make to all the families supported by the organization.

Find what rankles the CEO in your firm, and you'll have a leg up on figuring out your company's purpose. An example is Wal-Mart's purpose: "To give ordinary folks the chance to buy the same things as rich people." Sam Walton, founder of Wal-Mart, was bothered by the inequality between the rich and poor and had a passion for giving people in rural areas access to reasonably priced retail goods.

Again, "Mastering the Core Values" chapter provides more detail on how to determine the company's Purpose and how to use it to create a stump speech the leadership team can use to ignite employees' hearts.

Under the Purpose on the OPSP, you'll see an "Actions" section. It's easy for companies to create a list of Core Values, Purpose, and BHAG®, and then forget them. This "Actions" box is meant to drive a quarterly conversation about what's necessary, in the short run, to keep these long-term Vision items alive in the company and generate a handful of actions to bolster these core elements.

We had a client with a Core Value that emphasized the importance of having some "serious fun" as part of its culture. Having just gone public (which is no fun), the executive team decided at the next quarterly planning session to present the employees with a foosball table as a symbol that they didn't want to lose this fun aspect of the culture just because they were now part of a public company.

This is the kind of specific action item you would list under "Actions" in the Purpose column—specific ways to reinforce the Core Values, Purpose, and BHAG® in the next 90 days.

The Profit per X is a single KPI that represents the company's primary economic engine or Economics of One Unit (EOU) (e.g., the driving element of the business model). Southwest Airlines, for example, has a relentless focus on profit per airplane vs. other airlines' focus of profit per seat or profit per mile. The BHAG® represents the quantifiable 10- to 25-year target that aligns with the Purpose and Profit per X.

The key is for everything to align in column 2 and tell a compelling story that excites and engages the people to scale up the business. For a moving example, watch the five-minute, 25th-anniversary video tribute to Southwest Airlines' employees featuring then-President, CEO, and Chairman Herb Kelleher.

OPSP Column 3:
Targets, Sandbox, and Brand Promises

As we move to column 3, the plan becomes more detailed, listing specific financial targets and priorities over the next three to five years.

The first decision is choosing whether to look ahead three, four, or five years. The key question to ask is, "In what time frame do we plan to double the revenue/size of the company?" If the plan is to grow at 15%

per year, then you'll double in five years. If it's 25% per year, then choose a three-year time frame. If you're growing 100% per year, then your company is living in "dog years," when one year is like three to five for everyone else. In this case, choose a one-year time frame for column 3, a quarterly time frame for column 4, and a one-month time frame for column 5 (your month is like everyone else's quarter).

Since everything between the BHAG® and the next 90 days is a WAG (wild-ankle guess), the three- to five-year financial targets might as well be aspirational and aggressive. Specifically, looking at the top of column 3:

1. **Future Date**: Set the ending date for this medium-term planning period (e.g., 31 Dec 2028).
2. **Revenues**: Consider hitting a target revenue that's twice what it is today. Again, this is the definition of a camp on the way to your Everest: the point at which you're going to double the size of the business next.
3. **Profit**: Consider targeting three to five times industry average profitability. This is the definition of a great vs. good company, so go for it!
4. **Mkt. Cap/Cash**: If you lead a public company, set a goal for what the company will be worth (market cap). If you're at a private company, set a target for how much cash you would like to have in the bank or the market share you'd like to own within your industry.

Next, summarize the **Sandbox** in which the company plans to play over the next three to five years. It's a short buyer persona description of the core customers (Who and Where) and What it is you plan to sell them.

Then jump to the bottom of the column and clearly articulate the key needs you're going to satisfy for this Sandbox: the measurable **Brand Promises**. Note these specific metrics in the **Brand Promise KPIs** (Kept Promise Indicators) box. Rackspace measured Fanatical Support in terms of answering customer calls within three rings. FedEx's promise of 10 a.m. delivery and Oracle's Exadata 5x promise are additional examples of Brand Promise KPIs.

Once you've decided on the financial targets, Sandbox, and Brand Promises, choose the three to five Key Thrusts/Capabilities the company must pursue over the next three to five years. These might include a number of important acquisitions or the launch of a new product or service line. They might also represent a dramatic refocus of the core business, like Steve Jobs' decision, when he became Apple's CEO in 1997, to pull it out of all of its current business lines and focus on producing just two desktops and two laptops.

For Scaling Up, some earlier Key Thrusts/Capabilities included international expansion outside of the US and Canada; the launch of a software-as-a-service offering to support our methodologies; the creation of a high-end membership organization; a significant global expansion of our coaching organization; and the creation of an online learning platform.

These examples represent the kinds of significant medium-term priorities that a company should list in column 3 and are meant to provide a clear strategic direction for the next several years. To support the company's efforts, assemble a board of advisors. Recruit the smartest people you can find to advise you on each Key Thrust/Capability. It's always helpful to learn from those who have already been Where you're about to go.

OPSP Column 4: Goals

Moving to column 4, What are the #1 Priority and Key Initiatives for the company year—sometimes referred to as OKRs (Objectives and Key Results)? Addressing this starts with setting some very specific and expanded financial outcomes at the top of the column. Feel free to edit or add to the categories listed (e.g., some of you might not have significant inventory; tracking staff utilization instead might be more appropriate).

Next, jump to the bottom of the column and determine THE **Critical Number** for the year: "the main thing that will be the main thing." Yes, we recognize that your metrics are all critical, but this Critical Number designation is specific to one metric each year. "Mastering the Quarterly Theme" chapter will walk you through this Critical Number decision for the year and for the next 90 days (columns 4 and 5) and explain how to set Critical Number targets: Super Green, Green, and Red. Think of them as giving your team the chance to earn a gold, silver, or bronze medal this coming year.

In general, you'll pick a Critical Number that will address either an opportunity or a challenge on the **People/Balance Sheet** side of the business (e.g., reduce employee turnover, improve customer service scores, or dramatically reduce a credit line with the bank) or the **Process/ Profit & Loss** side (e.g., improve gross margins, reduce production cycle time, or increase sales close ratios). And depending on which side you choose, you will want to pick a counterbalancing number from the other side to monitor (e.g., you want to improve relationships but don't want to give away the store, or you want to improve processes but not damage relationships along the way).

Last, move to the middle of the column and ask, "What are a handful of Key Initiatives we must complete this year to achieve our financial outcomes and hit our Critical Number?" Think of these initiatives as your corporate New Year's resolutions (Less is more) and plan to revise them each time you close the books on your fiscal year—or as the marketplace demands—while keeping an eye on the longer-term goals.

These are NOT a random set of priorities. Choose them to achieve the Critical Number. The "Organizational Alignment" chapter will provide more details.

OPSP Column 5: Actions

Column 5 mirrors column 4, only it details *How* you're going to contribute this quarter to accomplishing the one-year goals, driven by the Critical Number and Rocks for the next 90 days. Given this short time frame, leadership should have sufficient clarity and foresight to set financial outcomes precisely (at the top of the column) and a Critical Number (at the bottom of the column) that the company can achieve.

KEY: The quarterly Critical Number represents a key step in achieving the annual Critical Number. For instance, Verne's brother-in-law worked for a company that set a specific cash target for the year. He then chose a Critical Number in process improvement for the quarter. The goal was to reduce the dollars spent on parts to repair machines, therefore saving significant money for his division and contributing to the cash goal.

Last, choose a handful of Rocks*—priorities that must be accomplished to achieve the quarterly financial outcomes and Critical Number. Again, less is more. Finally, place the initials of the person accountable for each Rock in the small corresponding "Who" box.

Think of these Rocks as a series of three to five simultaneous 13-week sprints that provide focus and direction to the rest of the organization.

*Rocks: This term honors the late Stephen R. Covey, author of *The 7 Habits of Highly Effective People: Powerful Lessons in Personal Change.* He would demonstrate how, if you have a limited amount of time (a bucket) and put in a bunch of pebbles first (email, distractions, etc.), there's not much room for the big important stuff (Rocks). But if you reverse the process—take care of the big things first—then there's room for all of it. To see an excellent demonstration of Covey's rock analogy, go to YouTube and search "Big Rocks in First" and watch the six-minute video with your team.

OPSP Column 6: Theme, Scoreboard Design, and Celebration/Reward

We will cover details for the Theme column, including some theme examples, in "Mastering the Quarterly Theme" chapter. To give you a quick overview, the idea is to build a fun and memorable theme around the Critical Number from the Quarterly column. Specifically, starting at the top of the Theme column 6:

1. **Deadline**: Normally the end of the current quarter.

2. **Measurable Target**: The quarterly Critical Number from the bottom of column 5.

3. **Theme Name**: Brainstorm a fun and relevant title for the Quarterly Theme. Current movie or song titles work well (*Fast & Furious* is always popular). Or try a play on a common phrase, like The City Bin Co.'s "Life Begins at 40" (the goal: generate 40,000 euros more in monthly earnings).

4. **Scoreboard Design**: It can be a hand-drawn chart on the wall or a whiteboard, or a more elaborately printed or electronic version. You ultimately want something visible so everyone can see the score, which is updated daily or weekly.

5. **Celebration**: The Quarterly Theme gives you a reason to host an event to either celebrate the accomplishment of a big goal or commiserate. It can be as simple as a barbecue in the parking lot, or it can be a significant trip. It is even more fun if you pick a celebration destination that aligns with the theme (e.g., a "Fast & Furious" theme culminates in a go-carting experience).

6. **Reward**: This might be prizes that align with the theme, or it can include a monetary incentive.

The key is giving your team finish lines and an opportunity to have some fun together.

OPSP Column 7: Your Accountability

Once the vision has been set, sit down with each individual or team in the company to establish what they can do over the next quarter to help the organization succeed. This creates "line of sight," through which everyone is able to see how his or her daily actions link to the company's goals. In some cases, doing a great job so that others are free to focus on a special initiative might be sufficient. Specifically, look at:

1. **Your KPIs**: Every employee or team should have an ongoing KPI or two that enables them to quantifiably answer the question, "Did we have a productive day or week?"

2. **Your Quarterly Priorities**: In addition to an individual's ongoing work, what are a few priorities for the quarter that will raise his/her performance or drive a special project that aligns with the employee's Critical Number and the #1 Priority of the company?

3. **Critical Number**: What is the single most important quantifiable quarterly achievement for that person or team that will help the company achieve its vision?

One of the keys to keeping people engaged is making a connection between their day-to-day efforts and the goals and vision of the company. If everyone can accomplish one thing in addition to his or her daily job, that's a dozen improvements every quarter, or hundreds, depending on the number of employees.

People and Process (Reputation and Productivity)

To realize a vision, you need people doing stuff! Otherwise, the vision is just words on a piece of paper. These two main components—People and Process—are listed just above the main body of the OPSP.

On the left side, we have listed the three main groups of People involved in any business: employees, customers, and shareholders. The goal is to continually improve the company's Reputation with all three as you balance the potentially competing demands between each group.

On the right side, we list the three main Processes that drive any business: Make/Buy, Sell, and Recordkeeping. The goal is to continually improve the company's Productivity in all three as you balance the potentially opposing demands between each process.

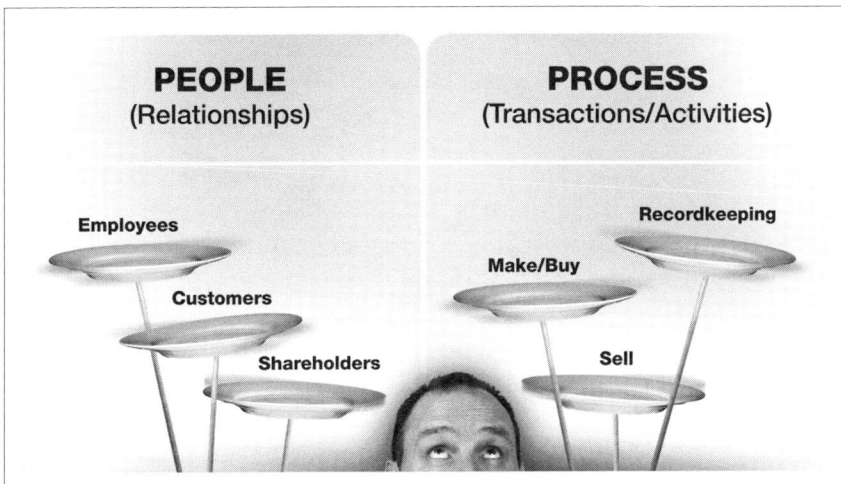

The big challenge is balancing the competing demands among all six, like maintaining spinning plates. You want to keep all the people happy (Reputation), but you can't give away the store (Productivity). You want to continually improve your Processes to drive better results, but you don't want to greatly upset any of the groups of People as you do so. Maintaining this balance between the demands of the People and Process sides of the business, as you scale up your Reputation and Productivity, requires frequent feedback and metrics to keep you from dropping any plates.

To complete the top portion of the OPSP, choose one or two KPIs you can track weekly to monitor the company's Reputation with all the stakeholders and the Productivity of the three main processes.

Here are some suggestions:

Employees: Happiness and engagement scores (TINYpulse and 15Five have simple systems for tracking these)

Customers: Kept Promise Indicators and Net Promoter System scores

Shareholders: Cash and company valuation

Make/Buy: Speed of processes (Lean), costs, and quality measurements

Sell: Close ratios, sales cycle, and revenue metrics

Recordkeeping: Relevance, speed, and accuracy of data

A Better Balance

The Balanced Scorecard™, popularized by Robert S. Kaplan and David P. Norton in their book by the same name, has been an industry-standard performance management tool for more than two decades. We align with Kaplan and Norton on the People side of the equation, emphasizing the need to balance the demands of employees, customers, and shareholders equally. Where we diverge is on the Process side. Kaplan and Norton lump all the processes into a single fourth category, whereas we break it into its three components: make/buy, sell, and recordkeeping. We believe this adds balance to the People side of the business. In the end, they balance four components, while we balance six.

Many nonaccountants struggle with understanding the basic functions and structures of a balance sheet and an income (profit & loss) statement. Considering the People and Process sides of the business from an accounting perspective often gives them a better grasp.

Let's look at the People side of the business. Track how the cash flows through the business with this equation:

Customers: Cash from anyone who pays you

minus (-)

Employees: Cash to anyone you pay ("employ"),
such as traditional employees, contractors,
suppliers, partners, banks, etc.

equals (=)

Shareholders: What is left to pay back investors,
banks, sweat equity, etc.

The balance sheet simply documents who owes you, whom you owe, and what is left over. It also notes how much cash you have. The goal is to generate sufficient cash to fuel growth as the company faces the First Law of Business Dynamics: Growth sucks cash!

Now let's look at the Process side of the business. Track how the business generates profit through these factors:

Make/Buy: The processes that generate expenses
Sell: The processes that generate revenue
Recordkeeping: The processes for tracking all of these transactions

The profit & loss (P&L) statement simply documents the revenue and expenses and determines if there is a profit. The goal is to abide by the Second Law of Business Dynamics: Buy low, sell high!

What's sad is that companies unknowingly violate this fundamental every day. It's why the #2 weakness of growing companies is the lack of sufficient financial data. You need data detailing the profitability of every customer, product, service, money, location, etc., so you can see where the business is making money and where it is not.

In the end, the financial goals of the company are to collect cash from customers fast enough to pay everyone it needs to employ and to reward the shareholders—and to sell things for more than they cost in order to generate a sufficient profit. Leaders must manage this balance between generating Cash and Profit, which mirrors the equilibrium between keeping the People happy and the Processes productive.

Preparing for a Strategic Planning Session

To complete the OPSP, JSJ Corporation finds that surveys are valuable tools. When it comes time to do a SWOT analysis, JSJ goes straight to its customers for feedback that influences its planning decisions. And to make the right calls about talent development, the company surveys its employees for insight.

CEO Jacobson believes that giving his team a chance to step back from the business and get reinspired has been vital to its planning process. JSJ typically sends its leadership team and members of its business team to our spring and fall ScaleUp Summits. JSJ's senior team arrives a day and a half early to do a deep dive into the OPSP and make updates. "It forces a discipline of getting away and taking the time to think deeply," says Jacobson.

To mirror JSJ's routine, there are four main activities in preparing for a strategic planning session (quarterly or annual):

1. Leaders at all levels gather feedback from employees and customers.
2. Team leaders complete a SWOT analysis and submit a Top 3 Priority list.
3. Senior leadership completes a SWT analysis and submits a Top 3 Priority list.
4. Everyone aims to keep learning and growing as a team.

Nothing can emerge from the collective brain of the team that doesn't enter it first. JSJ sparks via our online "company university" called the Growth Institute, the reading and executive education delivered in Scaling Up's book club and participation in our Scaling Up Summits. It also taps into the many decades of experience that company employees have accumulated.

Employee and Customer Feedback

The first preparatory activity is to send out a short Start/Stop/Keep survey to all the employees:

1. What do you think [company name] should **start** doing?
2. What do you think [company name] should **stop** doing?
3. What do you think [company name] should **keep** doing?

These are broad enough to solicit responses ranging from "We need a new microwave in the break room" to "We need to more fully utilize AI to streamline customer service."

Ask the same three questions of your customers. It could be a random sample if you have thousands of retail customers; or it might be more appropriate to have account managers query business-to-business customers face-to-face or over the phone. Use your best judgment, but be sure to incorporate customer feedback into the process.

The weekly routine of collecting and reviewing ongoing feedback from customers and employees will also feed into the decisions made during the planning process.

SWT and SWOT

We've observed for decades how market-leading firms eventually fall behind start-ups because they are blinded by their current reality. This is what Harvard Business School professor Clayton M. Christensen labeled the "innovator's dilemma" (detailed in his book by the same name).

So why do leaders miss seeing sweeping global trends that are about to broadside them? We put a big part of the blame on the standard SWOT analysis. It's time to update this methodology.

Inside/Industry Myopia

Almost by definition, the SWOT process drives leaders to look inward at both their company and industry challenges, creating what we term "inside/industry myopia." The traditional SWOT analysis, while helping executives see the forest and the trees, tends to lead them to forget that there's a world outside the forest. The SWOT, with this introspective focus, isn't the right tool to spot the trends in other industries and distant markets that CEOs must factor into their plans.

We don't want to throw away the SWOT. It still has its place in the strategic planning process. It's an excellent tool for gathering ideas and input from team leaders, who are more internally focused and closer to the day-to-day operations of an organization.

SWT Instead

For senior leaders, we propose replacing the SWOT with the SWT: an updated approach that identifies inherent *Strengths* and *Weaknesses* within their firms while exploring broader external *Trends* beyond their own industry or geography.

The *strategic planning* process comprises two distinct activities: — *strategic* thinking and execution *planning*. Strategic thinking is coming up with a few big-picture ideas. Execution planning is figuring out how to make them happen.

The traditional SWOT is a great tool for execution planning—the focus of middle management—resulting in a laundry list of accolades and fixes. However, for the senior team, the SWOT can be a trap. It tends to pull executives down into operational issues, distracting them from the much bigger forces around the globe that can take the company by surprise if it is not prepared.

It's Time to Build

Marc Andreessen, co-founder and general partner of Silicon Valley's premier venture capital firm Andreessen Horowitz (known as "a16z"), penned a blog at the beginning of the pandemic titled "It's Time to Build."

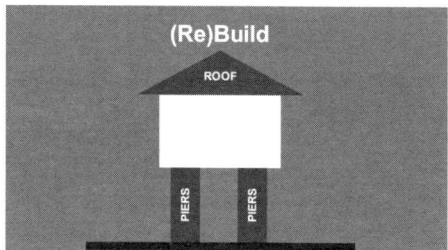

The piece was so well received and timely (we promoted it!) that a16z changed its tagline from "Software is eating the world" to this phrase. And we grabbed ahold of this idea of building to serve as an analogy for the pivots many companies need to continue to make with their business models and markets—build, rebuild, build, rebuild—as they move from plan A to Z.

Taking the building model literally, there are two components critical to success: laying down a rock-solid foundation and getting the roof on as quickly as possible. Then you can take your time completing the rest, knowing it's built to last.

This is the role of the SWT. It starts with a deep understanding of your organization's core Strengths (core competencies) and core Weaknesses—the foundational piers, anchored in bedrock, upon which the rest of the plan is built.

Next the roof. Actually, you want to get on the roof! You want to see over the forest and the trees of your industry and look to the horizon for tidal waves coming your way. It's important you recognize and get ahead of these market forces or Trends, so your firm is prepared to ride them successfully vs. get washed over by them.

Therefore, to anchor strategic thinking, senior leaders need to complete the SWT. It will help them face the brutal facts about the company's inherent strengths and weaknesses, and the global trends threatening to wash over their industry.

Let's look at the components of the SWT.

Trends

In addition to sizing up the immediate opportunities and threats that the SWOT tends to surface, the senior team needs to rise above all of this. Leaders should look at major trends, such as significant changes in technology, distribution, product innovation, markets, and consumer and social developments around the world that might shake up not only the business but the entire industry.

Forget about the competitor down the street. Is there a company on the other side of the globe that might put you out of business? Is there a new technology coming onto the start-up scene that could lead to an overnight change in the way all companies must do business? How is robotics changing the very nature of work? These are the kinds of questions the strategic thinking team must explore.

Choose four to six trends most likely to shake up your industry and business, and list them on the bottom of the OPSP. Recalling

Jim Collins' dual dynamic, mentioned earlier, these trends are meant to anchor the "stimulate progress" right side of the OPSP.

To up your game in seeing trends, we encourage each senior leader on your team to attend one tradeshow a year in an industry that couldn't be more different from your own. If you're in a heavily industrial business, choose a consumer industry show (someone on your team, no matter the industry, should attend the Consumer Electronics Show!). If you're in manufacturing, attend a professional services show. Mix it up and see what ideas you can shamelessly steal from another industry and install in yours.

To further stimulate your thinking, we recommend reading Peter Diamandis's book *Abundance: The Future is Better Than You Think* and attend his annual A360 conferences. In addition, Frost & Sullivan's team of futurists publish annual "Mega Trends" insights for various industries. Acquire the one for your industry and a few others.

Core Strengths and Weaknesses

Like you, an organization has innate strengths and weaknesses. Coping with them is less about changing who you are and more about leveraging the hand you've been dealt with (evolution!). Play to your strengths and avoid your weaknesses.

Core Strengths, often called Core Competencies, are a handful of resources and capabilities that anchor a firm's strategic advantage in the marketplace and emerge over time. In "The Core" chapter we shared BIC corporation's core competencies, which have allowed it to pivot beyond pens into lighters, razors, and other consumer products. We encourage you to read the famous *HBR* article titled "The Core Competence of the Corporation" by Gary Hamel and C.K. Prahalad. You can also Google for a myriad of examples from various firms.

Core Weaknesses, on the other hand, are attributes of an organization that are inherently weak and not easily fixable (and you shouldn't try to fix!). Many are cultural and foundational in nature. 3M, for instance, has a core weakness around selling direct to consumer pre-

cisely because it's such a "science" culture (its tagline is "Science."—with science being one of its two core strengths). Scientists like to innovate more than "sell," especially to the public.

To offset this lack of a direct sales culture, 3M developed a Core Strength around partnering, measured by the number of annual partner and "supplier of the year" awards the company receives. 3M serves as the science partner to thousands of companies, helping them innovate solutions to tough industry challenges—with over 60,000 solutions to date. These companies, in turn, help distribute these solutions.

Verne helped his children's international school, Ben Franklin International School (BFIS), discern their core strengths and weaknesses as part of a five-year strategic plan he was asked to facilitate. After months of "council" meetings held each week over lunch in the Head of School's office, the group concluded that the school's location in Barcelona was a key strength.

Being one of the most attractive cities in the world to live, especially for expats from Silicon Valley (Barcelona is the San Francisco of Spain, with 300 days of sunshine), BFIS was able to focus its recruiting efforts in the Bay area of the U.S. This was helpful because it offset a weakness of being in Barcelona. Most international schools pull students from the families of expats working in the overseas offices of Fortune 500 firms or government agencies/embassies. Those are all in Madrid.

In turn, BFIS's physical location was a weakness because there was no adjacent land near the school for expansion. Though the school had contemplated moving many times, during this planning cycle it chose to accept its location as a structural reality and to limit the number of students it could accept. BFIS also partnered with competitive schools nearby to use their sports facilities.

Like trends, the core strengths (core competencies) and weaknesses need to be identified as part of building a successful long-term plan and anchoring the base (along the bottom) of the OPSP. Given the relative long-term permanence of core strengths, they anchor the "preserve the core" side of the OPSP, on the left.

Mining All Levels

In summary, to feed the strategic planning process properly, the key is using different techniques to mine ideas from all levels of the organization. With frontline employees and customers, ask the Start/

Stop/Keep questions. With middle management, require a standard SWOT and inquire about their top three priorities for the quarter or year.

And demand that the senior team go deeper and broader using the SWT. Knowing what trends are going to shake up your industry—and having a plan for dealing with them—will help you stay ahead of the competition, and sniff out new rivals who want to take over your turf while you can still do something about it. At Amazon, one of the questions founder Jeff Bezos asked his team each week is what competitors have entered their market in the last seven days!

Doing the Right Things Right:
Your Completed One-Page Strategic Plan

Congratulations, you've completed the One-Page Strategic Plan, SWT, and Vision Summary! One caution—resist the temptation to go back and revise or wordsmith your document. The point isn't finding the exact words or using them perfectly. It's having something on a single sheet of paper that says it all for your company, no matter how imperfectly, and being able to use it daily to help your company reach its potential.

I've said it so often that I finally made it the headline above every One-Page Strategic Plan I distribute: You must remember that this process is 1 percent vision and 99 percent alignment. The lion's share of your effort must go not into meeting, talking, and wordsmithing, but toward getting your people aligned to do what needs to be done. Use your One-Page Strategic Plan and Vision Summary daily, weekly, quarterly, and annually to "Do the right thing!"

For details on how to prepare for and lead a strategic planning session along with a sample One-Page Strategic Plan (OPSP) go to www.scalingup.com and click on the "Free Chapters" link next to the picture of the books in the banner.

And to support implementation of the OPSP we have a SaaS tech platform called Align/Scoreboard that replaces a bunch of cascading excel spreadsheets with a mobile-ready application that helps everyone track and update their KPIs and Priorities (OKRs).

Start to Scale

EXECUTION

7

ORGANIZATIONAL ALIGNMENT AND FOCUS

Know your top priorities!

Executive Summary: The old saw is true: An organization with too many priorities has no priorities. This chapter will emphasize the need for leadership to clearly articulate to employees the three to five most important priorities that must be addressed or achieved to move the company to the next level. It's then critical that everyone in the organization determine his or her own Top 3-5 priorities, aligning them with the company's and creating the clarity that's crucial for top performance. In addition, this chapter will emphasize the need for additional clarity around the Top 1 of 5—the number-one priority that supersedes all others.

Have you ever noticed the lengths to which we human beings will go to avoid doing what needs to be done? There's no better time for cleaning the office than just before a big project or presentation is due. And who better to begin organizing the family photo album than the person who was supposed to be bringing order to the hall closet? It's just the way we are. We put lots of energy into avoiding the hard, unpleasant, realities of life. It's not that we don't know what to do. It's that we don't do it. This chapter emphasizes leadership's need to clearly articulate to employees the three to five most important priorities that must be addressed or achieved to move the company to the next level. It's then critical that everyone in the organization determine his or her own Top 3-5 priorities, aligning them with the company's and creating the activity plan that's crucial for top performance.

Consultant Ivy Lee visited Bethlehem Steel Company decades ago, long before it became the world's largest independent steel producer. "With our services, you'll know how to manage better," said Lee to CEO Charles Schwab. Schwab grew indignant. "What we need around here is not more knowing, but more doing! If you'll pep us up to do the things we already know we ought to do, I'll gladly pay you anything you ask."

Lee took him up on the proposition. "In 20-minutes," he told Schwab, "I'll show you how to get your organization doing at least 50 percent more." He started by having Schwab write down and prioritize his six most important tasks to complete in the next business day. Then he told Schwab, "Put the list in your pocket and take it out tomorrow and start working on number one. Look at that item every 15 minutes until it's done. Then move on to the next, and the next. Don't be concerned if you've only finished two or three, or even one, by quitting time. You'll be working on the most important ones, and the others can wait."

The consultant encouraged Schwab to share this approach with his executives, judge its value, and "send me a check for whatever you think it's worth." Two weeks later, Lee received a check for $25,000— a king's ransom in those days. In an accompanying note, Schwab said it was the most profitable lesson he'd ever learned. The lesson, of course, was the power of focus. The organization that understands— and acts upon—its Top 5 and Top 1 of 5 is the organization that progresses and prevails.

The key is not only making a list but identifying and working on the #1 priority first. Often, we'll get everything else completed on our list but the one we most need to do. I've also learned, after making a list the night before, that my perspective is different the next morning, after sleeping on it. So, review and reprioritize if necessary. Then make progress on your #1 each day.

Establishing a Planning Context for Your Top 5 and Top 1 of 5

In Chapter 6, the Planning Pyramid worksheet helped you align long-term goals with the quarterly challenges your organization faces. With these planning efforts in front of you, it's not hard to start figuring out what your Top 5 and Top 1 of 5 should be for the shorter term if you have sufficient market intel from your customers and employees.

Begin by asking yourself, what do I need to be doing *today* to keep this company moving towards its plans at the speed the market demands? Keep in mind your time frame, because these aren't necessarily annual priorities you're setting. Again, if you're growing 20–50 percent per year, a quarter equals a year. North of 100 percent growth, a month acts like a year.

Once you've determined your company's Top 5 and Top 1 of 5, each of your executives must determine his or her Top 5 and Top 1 of 5. Make the list the basis of a regular performance appraisal process. Continue to cascade this down the organization until you reach everyone. As you bring the process deeper into the organization and ratify it through the performance appraisal system, you're creating something magical called alignment. When you have everybody aligned, everybody at every level sees what you see and aspires to what you aspire. It's often helpful to hold a monthly or quarterly meeting of all your employees to review the firm's Top 5 and Top 1 of 5 priorities. Along with your core values, these priorities become the "handful of rules" that should drive decisions the next quarter. (Concrete tools for holding a successful quarterly meeting and driving quarterly priorities are provided in Chapter 7 Mastering the Quarterly Theme.)

But, to make your Top 5 and Top 1 of 5 something more than words on paper, to transform them into something achievable, you need a Management Accountability Plan or MAP *(Figure 7-1)*. Using this worksheet, you can assign the accountabilities necessary to get the job done. Don't dawdle on this. Within 24 to 48 hours of establishing your Top 5 and Top 1 of 5, determine who's going to be the point person on what, and when they'll produce the deliverables. We're talking accountabilities, sub-accountabilities, resource needs, deadlines, and sub-deadlines. It all goes in the Management Accountability Plan. Fill it out carefully and the result will be a week-by-week strategic plan over 13 weeks, detailing the steps that need to be taken and the milestones

Figure 7-1

M.A.P.
Management Accountability Plan

Accountable Team Member: _____

"Big Rock": _____

Goal Title: _____

Story: _____

_____

_____

	Actions	Who	When	Resources Needed
1st Qtr.				
2nd Qtr.				
3rd Qtr.				
4th Qtr.				
Next Year				
The Year After				

that must be reached to complete or make progress with this priority. Again, cascade this process down your organization, requiring everyone to produce a one page MAP for each of their major priorities.

Straightforward enough, right? Well, it isn't necessarily. Identifying and pursuing your Top 5 and Top 1 of 5 can be difficult and downright painful. If the process isn't at least making you uncomfortable, you probably haven't zeroed in on the right set of priorities, particularly your number one priority. We'll explore this subject next.

Recognizing Your Top 1 of 5: It's the One that Hurts

Perhaps the most outstanding example of how hard it can be to face and push through your Top 1 priority is golfer Tiger Woods. After winning the Masters in 1997, he was golf's golden boy—huge endorsement contracts and lots of press hype. Then he started losing, with people calling him a flash in the pan. For more than a year, he inexplicably failed to win anything. But then he became unstoppable, becoming the top-ranked golfer in the world from August 1999 to September 2004 (264 consecutive weeks) and again from June 2005 to October 2010 (281 consecutive weeks). During this time, he won 13 of golf's major championships. Tiger revealed to the world how he did it.

Tiger Woods had spent a long and agonizing year re-learning how to swing the club. He had realized that he would never achieve his goal of being golf's all-time greatest if he didn't adjust his swing, his number one and most difficult priority. For a while, the results were disastrous, but he endured. Tiger Woods had taken an unblinking look at himself and saw what was lacking. He recognized his Top 1 of 5, and he did what was required to face reality and push through the pain.

Seven Sore Points for Companies

In this last section of the chapter, I'll share with you seven common leading priorities and talk about how some companies I've worked with have addressed each. You'll find all seven in the Top 1 worksheet at the end of this chapter. You might want to keep a copy handy for easy reference.

Not big enough to compete

Often bigger is better. We have a manufacturing client that worked hard to improve its processes, respond to customer needs, build a great corporate culture, etc.—and each day the CEO knew in his heart he was sending his people up the hill to get slaughtered. He had a 10-ton gorilla of a competitor, and it was very clear to this leader that, long-term, the gorilla was going to win. As hard as this guy's people worked, all of his company's efforts would vaporize once the competitor threw money or manpower at the issue.

Reluctantly, this CEO acknowledged that it was never going to get any easier—until he himself became a 10-ton gorilla. He needed to merge with a bigger company.

My client sat, gave some thought to what might attract a buyer, and it became clear; he had to be the first in his industry to create a web-based solution. With that goal in mind—no small one, mind you—my client completely cleared his plate. For a year he did nothing but work with a programmer to get his company an online ordering system for a highly customized solution while the rest of his executive team ran the company. He built what became his industry's hottest trading site. And he reeled in the big fish he was looking for. He was able to successfully sell his firm to a 100-ton gorilla that made his competitor look like the small company his was before. This guy clearly recognized his number one priority, did what it took to complete it, and it paid off.

The company lacks a key player

One of the most danced-around issues in growing companies is personnel. How many times have we seen a company outgrow longtime players, yet instead of making the necessary personnel changes to strengthen their areas of responsibility, the CEO just starts growing redundant bureaucracy around the deadwood? It happens a lot and it holds a company back. Make replacing those people your number one priority now.

Perhaps the CEO wears too many hats. One firm I worked with desperately needed a CFO, but the founder-CEO just couldn't bring himself to pay the necessary salary to bring in a qualified financial person. He preferred to stretch himself too thin, and the company's results showed it. Once a CFO was on board, the company returned to growth and profitability within months.

The last version I'll cite to you is perhaps the toughest one of all: the need to replace yourself. We all know that the skills required to start a company aren't the same ones required to run and expand a company. Even Bill Gates reached this conclusion. At a certain point, he recognized that Microsoft would most benefit from getting him back to the visionary, entrepreneurial role he plays best. CEO Satya Nadella has been successful in scaling Microsoft to only the third firm to cross $3 trillion in market value.

The economic engine is broken

Maybe you're in a stupid business. Maybe the economic model on which you founded the company no longer makes sense. Whichever; you just know that the company is never going to make any money and you're surely not going to make it up in volume. The venture capitalists call it a "living-dead" company, meaning it's good enough to survive, but it's never going to do great things. Time to get out.

Don't read on too fast! Even if you're thinking, "My company's not a living-dead company," stop and consider: Are there parts of your company, or products, that meet the definition? Again, the advice is simple: Get out. Make that tough decision (read poker phenom Annie Duke's book *Quit: The Power of Knowing When to Walk Away* for the courage and insight).

Someone else is controlling our destiny

It happens, unfortunately. Somebody gains control over a key component of your business. If it's not curtains for the company, it's certainly a crisis. When Yahoo! lost mindshare around the word "search" to Google, the game was over. The same thing happened to Donald Burr at PeopleExpress, the mid-eighties discount airline. When American Airlines developed the Sabre reservation system, and PeopleExpress couldn't keep up with the multi-tier structure, Burr found himself out of business four months later. The lesson is clear: If a competitor gets hold of a key relationship or patent or supply line or word in the minds of the market, you'd better have a good counter-move or you're in trouble. I discussed this in Chapter 5, which has to do with brand promises and controlling the choke point of your industry.

We need a war chest to compete

It's what you might call the FedEx dilemma. You just can't be a player in some industries unless you charge off the blocks fast and strong. I know the CEO of a startup telecommunications company who understood this well. Knowing his company couldn't continue to exist unless it very quickly grew to scale, this guy spent just about all of his waking hours for several months amassing capital. His work culminated in a $210-million financing deal that got him the war chest he needed to compete. It's often one of the best reasons to go public.

We can't raise money 'til we grow

On the flipside, here's a cautionary tale to keep in mind when seeking capital. One of our MBD companies was adamant that its Top 1 of 5 was the need to raise $10 million. The executive team devoted itself to the goal—which is good. But the execs also took their eyes off the operational ball– which is bad. The result? Flat sales for two quarters. The company's valuation sagged badly, and would-be investors headed for the hills.

The CEO made the tough decision to forget about raising money and focus on driving sales. He made everyone a salesperson, including himself and the CFO who was working on the fundraising front. For a solid three months, he had the executive team meeting daily and weekly in a war room setting to track progress. At the end of 90 days, the company posted a 40 percent increase in sales. That performance allowed the CEO and CFO to go out and resume raising money—this time at a much better valuation.

We've got to scale back or we won't survive

Here's another story from our MBD files. For the first several years of a retail mortgage company's existence, the CEO considered his Top 1 of 5 to be rapid expansion—more markets, more mortgage products, more locations, more people. Then one day a large segment of his industry collapsed, due to various structural changes. It was gone. The only reason that company is around today, several years later, is because this CEO made the immediate and wrenching decision to lay off 240 of his 300 people. For quite a while, he looked like a failure. But his willingness to retrench got him back to the break-even point, and it kept his company alive long enough to see his industry move forward again. Often CEOs aren't willing to make the necessary cuts fast and deep enough. Instead, the death is slow and painful.

All of these examples prove one thing that Tiger Woods can vouch for with confidence: Pursuing your Top 1 of 5 goal is probably the most distasteful, frustrating, and perhaps discouraging thing you'll ever confront. It's not something you'll take on lightly, and I'd advise you not to do it alone. Tiger needed the clear-eyed advice and support of his coach, Butch Harmon. You need similar wisdom and backing from a strong board member, mentor, or executive coach (Scaling Up has over 260 coaches to help). You'll be glad you made the effort. And your employees and investors will praise your gutsy leadership.

Top 1

What is your number one?

1. Simply not big enough to compete—need to merge with larger firm.
2. Lacking a key player—until this position is filled, a lot of other efforts are wasted.
3. Economic engine is broken—there is simply no way to make money given the way we're doing business.
4. Someone else is controlling our destiny—We've lost control of a key component of our business to a competitor.
5. We need $200-million war chest to get to a competitive scale.
6. Can't raise money until we get back on a growth path.
7. Must scale back rapidly to reach the break-even point and take another run at it.

8

QUARTERLY THEMES

Establish a reason to celebrate!

Executive Summary: A company's goals and priorities won't be successful in driving the organization if they're easily forgotten or ignored. Once you've established what's important for your workforce to accomplish in the next quarter or year, do something to help your associates make the necessary emotional connection that generates commitment. Through a variety of real-world examples, this chapter will help you create the necessary themes and images to bring any company campaign to life. You'll also learn how companies track progress and celebrate success. Finally, you'll gain access to two tools that will assist you in planning theme-related events that will reach the myriad employees you have to lead and inspire.

What separates a plan on paper from one that lives and breathes on its own? It's an idea, an image—in short, an organizing theme. That's what transforms a mere leadership goal into a company-wide mission. French CEO Hubert Joly, who turned around Best Buy, notes in his book *The Heart of Business* (I named it #1 in 2021) that you don't have a strategy unless you've named it!

This chapter will help you create the necessary themes and images to bring any company campaign to life. You'll also learn how companies track progress and celebrate success.

Great leaders have always understood the power of a theme. The Revolutionary War in the United States was organized around "No Taxation Without Representation!" and the Boston Tea Party became not just an event, but an enduring symbol. Martin Luther King

Jr. built his goal of a more just society around his "I Have a Dream" speech. Leaders intuitively understand what too many business executives have yet to learn, which is that it takes an idea or an image to anchor a message with its listening audience. To get people to storm the barricades on your behalf, give them a concept that connects not just with their heads but with their hearts.

This need to connect with the feelings and desires of your workforce is proven and well accepted. In their seminal book, *The Leadership Challenge*, authors Jim Kouzes and Barry Posner speak powerfully of the need for CEOs to "encourage the heart" when seeking organizational alignment. I've seen it in action. I witnessed Michael Dell of Dell Computer rally his troops against a challenge from Compaq. He didn't just declare war on Compaq; he made the whole office a war zone. He donned army fatigues, he strung camouflage netting throughout headquarters, and he addressed his sales and production squadrons as if briefing them for a mission of no return. Did it make a difference? How could it not have?

Around the same time, baby America Online was under attack by giant Microsoft. Then-President Ted Leonsis gathered his AOL workforce and unveiled a huge dinosaur named Microsoft. In the weeks that followed, the dinosaur moved around headquarters as a trophy for any office or division that had struck a blow against the dinosaur.

Using Priorities and Critical Numbers to Drive Your Theme

Good themes don't pop out of thin air. The most powerful are those anchored in quantitative goals—be they annual numbers for companies growing less than 15 percent per year, or quarterly numbers for companies whose growth rate is north of that. Refer back to your One-Page Strategic Plan. With plan in hand, take your top priority and align it with your Critical Number—that one key measurable that you want your organization to focus upon. Then brainstorm a theme to go with it. It ought to be something that will make the numbers memorable.

This doesn't have to be anything particularly grand. The CEO of one major company had his three major priorities—represented by three Critical Numbers—engraved into wristwatches that he passed out to his execs. Whenever they checked the hour, they were reminded of the goals and that time was passing. It was simple and effective. So was the Phillips Group's decision to hold a company-wide meeting out of the back of a truck parked at a loading dock. The theme for the quarter was operational excellence, so what better way to emphasize the unsung heroes of the operation than to have the meeting on their under-appreciated turf?

But if you can come up with a theme whose production values rival Cecil B. DeMille's, I say, go for it! The movie *Apollo 13* has served many firms well as an organizing theme, complete with the famous line "Failure is not an option." At Synergy Networks, CEO Mark Gordon wanted to drive quarterly profitability and he saw it improving in three stages. What's got three stages? A rocket, of course, so Gordon donned a rented spacesuit and flanked himself with a chart depicting the profitability goals as a three-stage rocket. As he exhorted his team to greatness, he tossed space-themed toys out into the audience.

One useful source of quarterly themes is your core values. Take one each quarter and use it to bring focus and improvement to a certain aspect of the business. It's an excellent way to audit the organization's culture and to reinforce the core values. And speaking of values, no matter what the theme for the quarter, it's useful to review the organization's core values at the quarterly meeting, relating each to the theme. In addition, if you're into employee and team recognition activities, there is no better category of awards than your core values.

However you choose to develop and present your theme, do it with your whole workforce in mind. Thanks to the work of Harvard psychologist Howard Gardner, we now understand that there are at least seven different forms of intelligence: Verbal/Linguistic, Visual/Spatial, Logical/Mathematical, Bodily/Kinesthetic, Musical/Rhythmic, Interpersonal, and Intrapersonal. Each comes with its own preferred way of learning. At the end of this chapter is a chart entitled "Multiple Intelligences Summary" detailing the traits common to each of these seven intelligences. When you plan a theme-related event, try to hit as many of these intelligences as possible. Include not just words and pictures, but sounds, smells, feelings, and opportunities to reason, figure, or relate.

Tracking Progress and Keeping Score

What makes a theme a mission rather than a mere event? Effective reinforcement does, and that can be achieved through publicly tracking progress and keeping score.

At Synergy Networks, Mark Gordon's three-stage rocket lost a stage each time one of his profitability goals was met. It was a visual reminder of both the goals and the theme. It didn't hurt employee attention span, either, that there was a payout for the workforce each time a stage fell away from the rocket.

For Sapp Bros. Leasing, a truck-leasing business striving for 100 new leases by St. Patrick's Day, the tracking method was a big poster featuring 100 shamrocks. Each time a new lease was signed, another shamrock would be numbered. Again, there was a monetary payout when the goal was reached.

Progress doesn't have to be numerically quantifiable to be real, however. Each time the dinosaur took up residence in a new department at AOL, employees knew the company had made inroads in its battle against Microsoft. It was their way of keeping score. In all cases, the symbol or scoreboard for the theme was highly visible. This isn't the time for 8.5" x 11" charts. Make them big, make them noticeable, make them memorable.

As you plan your visible tracking and scorekeeping, keep in mind this is an ideal opportunity to involve and engage some of the people who don't normally get involved in quarterly or annual goal achievement. At the trucking company, the shamrock chart was beautifully designed and executed by somebody in the front office with an artistic streak. Her efforts enhanced the experience for everybody, including herself. You have people in your organization that can do the same, and more. They're just waiting to be asked.

Rewarding and Celebrating

Reward is sometimes considered a dirty word. It's assumed that if there's a reward involved, it's somehow buying the workforce's participation. I don't see it that way. I think people need to know where they're going and they want to know when they've arrived. It's like reaching the last day of school. Remember how great that felt, taking the last test in the last class on the last day of school? If somebody gave you a gift to take home, that was wonderful, but the real rush was just getting to the end and knowing you'd done it. It's like that on the job, too. Nobody's going to turn down a hard-won bonus or prize, but that's just the frosting on the cake. The real reward is the sense of celebration that comes from reaching a goal and doing it together.

At McKinney Lumber in Alabama, retention was the goal. When retention reached one level, the leadership team hosted a hotdog roast. When it reached the next level, the fare was barbecued chicken. At the highest and final level, it was steaks for everybody, with the leadership team doing the cooking. Now, a free steak dinner is nice, but was it enough to buy the workforce's participation? Probably not. Dinner was provided to celebrate the achievement of a shared goal — and to mark the end of the quarterly campaign.

At Gorman's Business Interiors in Detroit, former CEO John Anderson devised Gormanopoly, a Monopoly-like game that gave teams points for "just about anything you could incentivize," as Anderson put it. There were points for profitability goals, for improved collection on receivables, for customer satisfaction, for health and fitness, for community service, you name it. The scoreboard consisted of three ships—one representing each team—moving across a board to the finish line. The reward, or celebration, was a Caribbean cruise for each team that satisfied the goal criteria.

All three teams made it in the first year the game was played and the company gladly footed the $32,000 cost of sending each employee and his or her guest on the trip. "It was a huge success," recalls Anderson. "Not only was it good for the organization, it got us good PR without a lot of promotion, customers got engaged in it and learned about our [company] culture, and it was a great recruiting tool, too."

Advertising and PR firm RMR and Associates used an all-inclusive trip to Montego Bay, Jamaica as its prize for its annual open-book leadership goal. CEO Robyn Sachs says, "How they earned it was by hitting a particular gross income number, $2.7 million in AGI. Well, we blew the number out. We got to $2.9 million and took about 50 people to Jamaica. It was great." She adds, "The goal gets people focused on the right things, but it's still just a game and it's fun. You get the whole company pulling together."

Sachs' company next played Stockopoly, "a stock-appreciation-rate scheme" as she calls it. The reward or goal this time is "cold, hard cash" and, although the game went well, Sachs says she's a tad disappointed.

"The Jamaica trip had more of an emotional pull on people than the money had," she says. "I'm starting to see that the trip got people more excited."

Maybe the lesson in these examples goes right back to the Kouzes-Posner book, *The Leadership Challenge.* The trick in developing a successful quarterly theme isn't just coming up with a good idea or presenting it well or tracking progress effectively or even celebrating. It's encouraging the heart. Only when we do that extraordinarily well do we experience extraordinary success. At the end of this chapter is a worksheet you can use to organize your quarterly theme rollout.

Multiple Intelligences and the Quarterly Theme

Intelligence	Activities	Materials	Strategies	Presentation Skill
Verbal/ Linguistic	*lectures, discussions, word games, storytelling, choral reading, journal writing, etc.*	*books, tape recorders, typewriters, stamp sets, books on tape, etc.*	*read about it, write about it, talk about it, listen to it*	*teaching through storytelling*
Logical/ Mathematical	*brain teasers, problem solving, science experiments, mental calculation, number games, critical thinking, etc.*	*calculators, math manipulatives, science equipment, math games, etc.*	*quantify it, think critically about it, conceptualize it*	*Socratic questioning*
Visual/ Spatial	*visual presentations, art activities, imagination games, mind-mapping, metaphor, visualization, etc.*	*graphs, maps, video, art materials, optical illusions, cameras, picture library, etc.*	*see it, draw it, visualize it, color it, mind-map it*	*drawing/ mind-mapping concepts*
Bodily/ Kinesthetic	*hands on learning, drama, dance, sports that teach, tactile activities, relaxation exercises, etc.*	*building tools, clay, sports equipment, manipulatives, tactile learning resources, etc.*	*build it, act it out, touch it, get a "gut feeling" of it, dance it*	*using gestures/ dramatic expressions*
Musical/ Rhythmic	*superlearning, rapping songs that teach*	*tape recorder, tape collection, musical instruments*	*sing it, rap it, listen to it*	*using voice rhythmically*
Interpersonal	*cooperative learning, peer tutoring, community involvement, social gatherings, simulations, etc.*	*board games, party suppies, props for role plays, etc.*	*teach it, collaborate on it, interact with respect to it*	*dynamically interacting with participants*
Intrapersonal	*individualized instruction, independent study, options in course study, self-esteem building, etc.*	*self-checking materials, journals, materials for projects, etc.*	*connect it to your personal life, make choices with regard to it*	*bringing feeling into presentation*

Quarterly Theme Meeting

Who's Accountable?

When will you hold the meeting?

Theme of meeting?

Using the Multiple Intelligences list of activities, what will you do at the meeting?

Verbal/Linguistic

Logical/Mathematical

Visual/Spatial

Bodily/Kinesthetic

Musical/Rhythmic

Interpersonal

Intrapersonal

9

MEETING RHYTHM

Structure meetings to enhance team performance!

Executive Summary: To make more than just a lot of noise in your business, you need rhythm – an effective meeting rhythm. And the faster you pulse, the faster you'll grow. At the heart of team performance is a series of tightly run daily, weekly, monthly, quarterly, and annual huddles and meetings—all of which happen as scheduled, without fail, with specific agendas. With these meetings you'll have opportunities to focus your team(s) on what's important and actually save people time during their day and week! You'll also solve problems more quickly and easily, you'll achieve better alignment around strategic decisions, and you'll communicate more effectively. This chapter details agendas, timing, and who should participate in each of these meetings.

Reading John D. Rockefeller's biography, *Titan*, I was struck by his daily luncheon habit. Each day, without fail, he'd sit down with his key people, have lunch, and talk. At first, the meetings included only Rockefeller and the four co-founders of Standard Oil. But as the decades wore on and the company grew, the meetings came to include Rockefeller's nine directors. And yes, they continued to meet daily.

Consciously or not, Rockefeller understood that the word company meant "to share bread." He knew that by gathering his top lieutenants and advisors each day for a meal, their personal and professional relationships would be strengthened. Fortified for another day, each could go out and do his share to conquer the oil industry or Wall Street or whatever the current target might have been. Did it matter that the meetings occurred daily? I'm confident Rockefeller would say an emphatic "Yes!"

A century later, the late Steve Jobs would do the same in turning around Apple. In addition to setting up a daily situation room to meet with the leaders of the four products (personal and corporate desktop, personal and corporate laptop) Apple would launch to re-establish their prominence in the computer industry, Steve would have lunch, daily, with Jonathan Ive, his head of design.

When Airbnb lost $1 billion of bookings at the beginning of the COVID pandemic in 2020, the leadership met daily seven days a week to power through the crisis. They continued the routine pre- and post-IPO.

Meetings: A Routine to Set You Free

In the 40 years I've spent working with growing companies, the predictable winners are those who have established a rhythm and a routine of having meetings. The faster they're growing, the more meetings they have. This may sound ludicrous to those of you who have worked for large corporations, where meetings are dreaded interruptions that eat up hours or even days. But I'm not talking about the kind of wide-open, poorly defined meetings many of us have endured. I'm talking about short, punchy meetings with a structure, time limits, and a specific agenda. This type of meeting doesn't leave you feeling bogged down. On the contrary! This type of meeting routine sets you free.

Think about jazz for a minute. Lots of freedom in that, right? At first glance, all you see is the improvisation. But if you study jazz or talk about it with somebody who really knows the idiom, you soon realize that there is a rock-solid rhythm and a set of rules underlying all that passionate free styling. To come together and create something amazing, all players must understand jazz's basic structure and agree to work within it (the core). They need to be competent musicians (A-players). They need to be on the same sheet of music – performing the same song (one-page plan). And they need to be playing to the same beat (rhythm). This is what separates great music from noise.

For growing companies, when meetings are the rhythm and agendas are the rule, pros and unknowns can come together to create something new and marvelous. New people (and even newly acquired companies) get up to speed quickly when there's an obvious structure they can align with.

More Frequent, Shorter Meetings

Quarterly and annual meetings are givens in most companies. At the quarterly, you measure progress toward a year-end goal. At the annual, you consider that progress and set new goals for the following year. The key agenda for these quarterly and annual meetings is based around the One-Page Strategic Plan (described in Chapter 6). That's all well and good. But I am adamant that you need to add daily, weekly, and monthly meetings as well. Why? Because the agendas of these more-frequent meetings drive the deliverables outlined in the less-frequent quarterly and annual strategic gatherings. Each one builds upon the next.

For example, how are you going to make your quarterly goals if you aren't driving performance monthly, weekly, even daily? Your teams need regular, face-to-face huddles to discuss new opportunities, strategic concerns and bottlenecks as they arise. Similarly, how many hours is it going to take to hammer out a set of goals for a new year, if the annual meeting is the first time anybody's talked about where the market's going or dealt with the tactical issues that come up weekly?

And the faster you're growing, the faster your meeting rhythm should pulse. In general, if you're growing less than 15 percent per year, you can treat the year like a year from a strategic thinking standpoint. If you're growing 20 percent to 100 percent a year, think of each *quarter* as if it were a year. That means plotting new strategy each quarter. If you're among the elite, more than doubling your revenue each year, you need to treat each *month* as if it were a year. For more discussion on this hyper-pulsing style of management, read the seminal book *Competing on Internet Time* by Michael Cusumano and David Yoffie. It outlines the browser battle between Netscape and Microsoft. Netscape sustained rapid and successful growth by treating each month as if it were a year. Growing faster than almost any firm at the time, Netscape nonetheless took its executives offsite each and every month to hold a formal strategic meeting. In so doing, Netscape didn't just talk the talk of pulsing monthly; they walked it.

Daily Meeting—An Imperative

Everyone in a growing company should be in some kind of five- to 15-minute huddle *daily*. I don't mean they all have to be in the same meeting, just in some meeting. To me, this is non-negotiable.

Of course, the immediate pushback I always get on this is, "We're too busy!" People moan and groan about how thinly they're spread, or how much they're traveling. They can't imagine finding the time to get everybody in the same place every day for 1 minute, let alone 5 or 15. Or, if the company is quite small and travel isn't that big an issue, they'll tell me, "We don't need a meeting when we're seeing each other all day long."

Each argument sinks of its own weight. First off, thank goodness for cell phones. The meeting doesn't have to be in your conference room or around somebody's desk. A conference call or Zoom session will do just fine when people are on the road. And what's five or 15 minutes? The equivalent of a bathroom break! Second, this stuff about working too hard or seeing each other too much already is besides the point. Casual encounters fail to take advantage of the three most powerful tools a leader has in getting team performance: peer pressure, collective intelligence, and clear communication. I'll elaborate a little right now; more later in the chapter.

These meetings save you time – you can figure every minute in a daily saving people ten minutes. Thus an 8-minute daily huddle saves everyone roughly an hour and a half each. By maintaining a rigorous daily meeting schedule, you'll always be able to find one another for a substantive consultation. If you need an answer to a customer question, you don't need to say, "I'll try to find her and get back to you sometime today." You can name the time, because you know you'll have the answer by the end of your daily meeting. Nor will you be going over the same water-cooler conversation three or four times, as is the case when you rely on chance hallway meetings for communication. Because everyone's together in a daily meeting, things get quickly and accurately communicated.

Equally important, in one-on-one meetings there is a lot of private negotiating going on ("You know what I'm up against...."), putting the leader in the constant position of being the bad gal or guy. However, by having everyone on the same call for a few minutes, it takes the heat off the leader and provides peer pressure that increases the rate of deliverables.

Last, a daily meeting focuses the collective intelligence of the team on the issues at hand. What a shame to have a high-powered exec team that doesn't take even 15-minutes each day or an hour a week to focus its horsepower on the opportunities at hand! Without the discipline I'm describing, don't kid yourself into thinking you're getting this focused collective power and attention.

Daily Meeting Structure

Focus
Top 1 Bottleneck

Quick Daily Agenda—5 to 15 minutes

2–5 minutes — What's up? Each person shares their #1 priority for the next 24 hours and specifics about activities, meetings, accomplishments, noteworthy news from customers, etc.

2–5 minutes — Daily measurements/indicators from each person—from the day before and their goal today.

2–5 minutes — Where are you stuck? Each person shares their specific barrier/constraint/bottleneck to accomplishing their priorities.

Optional — Review a core ideology.

Stand up, don't sit down, for a meeting.
By phone if only option.

When is your daily meeting going to be? _____

Who is going to attend? _____

Will it be a conference call or stand-up meeting? _____

Whose office? _____

Timing

To work well, the daily meeting must be set up right. I recommend that companies set the time a little irregularly—every day at 8:08 a.m. or 4:46 p.m. For whatever reason, people are more on time when the time's not on the half or quarter-hour. Worried that you'll forget the meeting? Set a daily alarm on your phone.

Make on-time attendance mandatory, with no excuses! I've been in intense meetings with clients. I've been in the midst of seeking funds from venture capitalists. It doesn't matter; I tell them I need to take a break for my daily meeting. And it only gains me respect.

Overall, start and end on time and don't problem solve. This meeting is simply for problem identification. And if it starts to go longer than 15-minutes, people will drop the habit.

Setting

Meet wherever you want, but I strongly suggest you avoid sitting comfortably. Stand up, or perch on stools. It'll help keep the meeting short. Gathering in the leader's office makes it easier for him or her. If via conference call, have everyone call/zoom in vs. a few standing around a conference bridge or desktop.

Who Attends

The general rule is, the more the merrier—though you may wish to alter the approach a little if the group gets quite large or far-flung.

The Ritz Carlton gathers about 80 headquarters personnel for a ten-minute daily huddle outside the CEO's office. Also, in every Ritz hotel from Bali to Boston, each employee who isn't on the desk or answering phones attends a daily shift meeting to discuss problems and reinforce company philosophy. Marriott has continued the practice since purchasing the Ritz.

Alan Rudy at Express-Med used daily huddles to keep his company pulsing, too. And because he had his people on multiple project teams, he began calling them all together for a single 15-minute meeting. For the first five minutes the project leaders report what was happening and describe any sticking points that developed. After that, everybody huddled up as needed. The beauty of Rudy's approach is that it got absolutely everybody out of his or her cubicle and involved. Where once a project leader had to seek out somebody whose task overlapped his or her own, the inevitable redundancies and cross-functional needs were now worked out almost immediately.

The most ambitious daily meeting schedule I know of belonged to The Scooter Store, a nationwide seller of motorized scooters, mainly for the elderly. The entire company re-aligned every 24 hours, through a rapid series of daily huddles. First, the frontline teams across the country huddled locally for 15 minutes. Immediately following that meeting, the leaders of those teams met on a national conference call for another 15 minutes. Last, the executive team met for a final 15-minute session. Across a mere 45 minutes each day, the entire company conferred—bottom to top.

Who Runs the Meeting

Pick someone who is naturally structured and disciplined, (and that might not be the CEO). Whoever it is, the main job is to keep things running on time. Use a countdown stopwatch to make sure you don't let any part of the agenda run away with the meeting.

The person running the meeting also has the important job of saying, "Take it offline." Whenever two or more people get off on a tangent that doesn't require everybody's attention, instruct them to continue the conversation outside the boundaries of the meeting.

The Agenda

The agenda should be the same structure every day, and it's just three items long: what's up, daily measures, and where are you stuck? In the first five minutes, each attendee spends a few seconds (up to 30) just telling what's up, especially their #1 priority for the day. That alone is valuable, since it lets people immediately sense conflicts, crossed agendas, and missed opportunities.

Next, the entire group takes a quick look at whatever daily measurements/KPIs your company uses to track its progress. (You do have some, don't you?) A digital retailer might track website hits. A sales organization might track the number of proposals that went out that day. Wal-Mart uses stock price. Also, choose a short-term employee-based activity you want to focus on and track daily. Maybe it's accounts receivable or getting contracts back on time. It ought to be some sort of measurable behavior.

The third and most important agenda item is where people are stuck. You're looking for bottlenecks, which ought to be your nemesis in business. Applying energy anywhere but the sticking point is a waste.

There are a couple of reasons why I consider this last part of the agenda crucial. First, there's something powerful in simply verbalizing—for the whole group to hear—your fear, your struggle, your concern. It's the first step in solving the problem, because until the mouth starts moving, the brain won't engage. Second, the bottleneck discussion often reveals who's not doing his or her job. Anytime somebody goes two days without reporting a sticking point, you can bet there's a bigger problem lurking. Busy, productive people who are doing anything of consequence get stuck pretty regularly. The only people who don't get stuck are those who aren't doing anything. So, scrutinize the team member who reports, "Everything is fine!"

This daily huddle agenda aligns with what the Gallup organization found is key to employee engagement. Employees want to be coached vs. managed. And the key coaching question is "what is your #1 goal and what's in your way of achieving it?" Daily, you'll hear the answers to this question and after several days (it takes 6 datapoints to establish a trend) you'll have several coachable moments. Are they working on the right thing? Important vs. urgent? And how might you help remove the barriers to accomplishing their #1 priority?

Important as it is, the bottleneck conversation shouldn't be allowed to drift into problem solving. It's okay if somebody wants to reply to a bottleneck by saying, "Call so-and-so," but anything more than that should be taken offline. Remember: The daily meeting needs to be kept short. At the end of this chapter is a one-page overview of the daily meeting agenda.

The Weekly Meeting Agenda

The weekly meeting has a different purpose, and therefore, a different agenda. It's intended to be a more issues-oriented and strategic gathering. It won't be, however, unless you've established your daily meeting rhythm. By holding daily meetings, you put out a lot of the fires and clear up a lot of the outstanding issues that would otherwise bog down the weekly meeting. That's the all-important synergy.

We label the weekly meeting a "4D Meeting." It's a 4D look at the organization representing the four steps/outcomes of an effective weekly gathering: Discover, Debate, Decide, and Delegate.

In the paragraphs that follow, I'll discuss some of the differences between the daily and weekly meeting agendas. See the back of the chapter for a complete agenda for the 4D weekly meeting.

The Schedule

Schedule the meeting for the same time, same place each week; 30 minutes for firstline employees and a full hour for team leads and execs. Again, it can be a Zoom call, as we do on Monday's at 9am EST, if your leaders work in different locations.

Five Minutes: Good News (Discover)

Each weekly meeting starts with five minutes of good-news stories from everyone. They include personal and professional good news, and the more fun the better. Laughter brings brains into an alpha state, the result being more effective meetings. This starts the meeting on a good note, focuses everyone on the positive and serves as a mental health check. If someone has gone a couple weeks without specific good news, the leader should intervene privately to see if everything is okay.

Ten Minutes: Customer and Employee Feedback (Discover)

Spend the next ten minutes reviewing specific feedback from customers and employees. (You do get this on a weekly basis, don't you?) What issues are cropping up day after day? What are people hearing? And you'll need to be gathering this input daily/weekly to have something to discuss. It's critical intel for driving decisions/priorities.

Ten Minutes: The Priorities and Numbers (Discover)

Spend ten minutes updating everyone on the progress of the quarterly priorities and individual and company-wide measures. Every firm should have key performance indicators I call Moneyball stats. These are usually ratios that provide true insight into the future performance of the business. And these measures should be displayed graphically (see the weekly meeting agenda at the back of the chapter). Our Scaling Up Scoreboard SaaS platform makes this easier to share and display key metrics.

30 Minutes: A Rock, or Single Issue (Debate/Decide)

The big mistake made at weekly meetings is covering everything every week. As a result, the team deals only with issues on a shallow level and never focuses its collective intelligence for a period of time on one issue. The key is focusing on a large priority for the month or quarter, what I described in Chapter 7 as Rocks. Firstline employees spend about ten minutes on this, while the executive team may devote as much as a half hour. And limit it to one topic. Attempt more, and nothing will get done. Which topic should be discussed? Choose one of the priorities you've established in your monthly or quarterly meetings, and plan that it should come up for discussion more than once a month or quarter. For example, if one of your priorities is to get an internal AI system up and running, the executive with accountability for that project should be in the hot seat at least two or three times over a 13-week quarter, just giving updates and getting feedback. By rotating the topics in this fashion, you'll knock out 15 to 20 rocks each year, you'll do it faster than you thought possible, and you'll feel less brain-dead doing it.

Who, What, When (Delegate)

At the end of the 30 minute discussion/debate, summarize Who is going to do What, When. This serves as the key notes from the meeting and assures someone has accountability for each of the deliverables decided by the team.

One-Phrase Close (Discover)

End your weekly meeting by asking each attendee to close with a word or phrase. How are they feeling about what was discussed or decided? It creates a formal closing for the meeting, it ensures that everyone's had a chance to say something, and it gives you a window on what people are thinking and feeling. If you find there are lingering issues or conflicts, you can follow up.

It's ideal if the weekly meeting is just before breakfast, lunch, or happy hour so the executives can have a more informal setting in which to discuss issues that surface during the structured part of the meeting. That informal time is often when real decisions are fleshed out.

The Monthly Meeting—Agenda Is Learning

If the focus of the quarterly and annual meetings is setting strategy and the focus of the daily and weekly meetings is execution, the focus of the monthly is on learning—a chance for the executive team to "pass its DNA" down to the next level. This is a two-hour to four-hour meeting (we take four hours) for the extended middle and senior leadership team to gather, to review the progress everyone is making on their priorities, to review the monthly P&L in detail, to discuss what's working and not working from a process standpoint, and to make appropriate adjustments. It's also a time to do an hour or two of specific training.

The key is to involve all senior and team leaders, giving them a structured time to work together. This is critical in growing the middle leadership team and keeping them aligned.

"Why So Many Meetings?"

Perhaps you've read this far thinking "We already do these things—either in our quarterly and annual meetings, or one-on-one. We don't need all this extra structure." Let me take one more crack at convincing you, starting with the one-on-one issue.

Daily and weekly meetings are demonstrably superior to one-on-one sessions. In one-on-ones, there's no Greek chorus singing out when the untruths begin to fly. People will give one person excuses that they'd never try before an entire group, where confrontation is likely. Where goals are at stake, and accountability is an issue, the peer pressure of the daily and weekly meetings keeps things moving much better than if an individual exec is reporting to the CEO. Why? Because it's just easier to get the job done than to have to face the team each day, each week, and make the same excuses for having failed to get it done. So, meetings increase the pace of deliverables, and, not incidentally, take lots of time pressure off the top leader.

I'm also sold on the value of the collective intelligence that gets harnessed in daily and weekly meetings. Just as the audience lifeline in the television game "Who Wants to Be a Millionaire?" is consistently more accurate than the phone-a-friend lifeline (the equivalent of a one-on-one), getting your entire team's brains focused on an issue is much more effective than focusing one-on-one. A side benefit, of course, is the opportunity these daily and weekly meetings afford you to reinforce your core ideologies and give pats on the back.

Sure, you can continue holding your meetings only monthly, quarterly, and annually without the daily and weekly huddles. If you make your monthly and quarterly meetings more strategically oriented, you'll feel you're doing a wonderful job of keeping up with the breakneck pace of change. But here's my question: as fast as you're pulsing, what makes you so sure you're not headed somewhere you don't want to go? Certainty comes with routine, with rhythm, and yes, with daily and weekly meetings.

4D Weekly Meeting Structure

Relevancy. Set a time each week to focus on what's important. It may seem impossible at first, but once the habit is created and the meeting is structured properly, most people will look forward to the meeting and find they can't function properly without it. These employee team meetings are *the* major building block for implementing the rest of the ideas you are learning in this book.

To make these meetings productive and useful, I suggest using the following suggested agenda. I also recommend you have the meeting right before a critical time deadline, like lunch or 5:00 p.m. or 8:00 a.m. This will cause the meeting to end on time.

Suggested Agenda

5 minutes—Good News. Go around the group and have everyone share two good news stories, one personal and one business, from the past week. This is a way to counter the negativity of these meetings, since they are mainly focused on addressing challenges, and a way to help people begin to see the good, not just the bad. It's also a great way to get to know each other better and to give each other pats on the back. This may feel awkward at first, but make sure everyone participates.

10 minutes—Customer and Employee Data. Go over the basic logs. Again, don't get hung up in conversation. Just review whether there are any recurring issues or concerns that the team or its customers are facing day in and day out. Choose one issue and assign a person or small group to explore it to get to the root cause.

10 minutes—The Numbers. Go over everyone's individual or team weekly measures of productivity. Don't get hung up in conversation. Just report the numbers. It's best if the numbers are displayed graphically. It helps people see trends in the data.

10 to 30 minutes—Collective Intelligence. Open the conversation around a rock—a large priority. Use the collective intelligence of the team to drill into a big issue. Have the person with accountability for a rock make a presentation on how they are addressing it.

One-Phrase Closes. Go around the room and let everyone say a word or phrase that represents how they feel at that moment about the meeting.

Keep a Log. Record *who* said they would do *what, when.*

This 30- to 60-minute meeting each week, if effective, will help make everyone's job easier and more productive. If it doesn't, reexamine how the meeting is being run and what is being discussed, but don't quit this crucial rhythm.

Start to Scale

CASH

10

CASH FLOW

*Improving the cash conversion cycle
of the business model*

Executive Summary: Cash is the oxygen that fuels growth. And the cash conversion cycle (CCC) is a key performance indicator (KPI) that measures how long it takes for a dollar spent on anything (rent, utilities, marketing, payroll, etc.) to make its way through your business and back into your pocket. In this chapter, we'll share several ways that companies have dramatically improved their CCC using the one-page Cash Acceleration Strategies (CASh) tool, allowing them to fund growth with internally generated cash and freeing them from the grasp of banks and/or investors. We suggest that you brainstorm ways to improve cash flow at each 90-day planning session and pick a related initiative as one of your handful of priorities each quarter. Constantly improving the cash flow of the company—and better understanding how cash moves through the business—is a powerful driver for improving the firm as a whole

When Michael Dell was growing his company rapidly, he reached a point in the mid-'90s when he ran out of cash. He was "growing broke," like so many other businesses scaling up quickly. That's when he brought in Tom Meredith as CFO. Meredith calculated Dell Inc.'s cash conversion cycle (CCC) to be 63 days. That meant it took 63 days from the time Dell spent a dollar on anything until it flowed back through the business and onto the balance sheet (into the bank) as cash.

Focusing on one cash improvement strategy/initiative each 90 days, Meredith drove the CCC to negative 21 days by the time he left Dell as CFO a decade later. This meant the company received a dollar 21 days before it had to be spent on anything. As Dell grew faster, it generated cash instead of consuming it. That is why the founder and CEO had sufficient cash to contribute to taking the company private in 2013 (and back public in 2018, netting him $50 billion in what Forbes named the "Deal of the Century" in 2021).

In this chapter, we'll examine strategies for accelerating your cash flow through improvements in your CCC.

Cash Conversion Cycle (CCC)

Not every business can have a negative CCC, but you can view Dell's example as inspiration to move yours in that direction. It is just a matter of looking for ways to improve it. For instance, Catapult Systems LLC, an Austin-based, Microsoft-focused IT consulting company, used to bill clients on a 30-day cycle. Meanwhile, employees were paid twice a month, leading to what founder and Chairman Sam Goodner calls "a terrible cash-flow story." He simply started billing his clients twice per month, after finding more than 90 percent were agreeable to the change. This nearly doubled cash flow immediately.

To tackle the cash conversion cycle, start by reading "How Fast Can Your Company Afford to Grow?" a *Harvard Business Review* article by Neil C. Churchill and John W. Mullins. It provides the formulas to help your team calculate the company's overall CCC and discusses many of the financial levers highlighted in the last chapter of this "Cash" section of the book.

NOTE: John Mullins, serial entrepreneur and London Business School professor, subsequently wrote a book titled *The Customer-Funded Business: Start, Finance, or Grow Your Company with Your Customers' Cash*. The title says it all! Read it for an advanced look at the cash side of your business and for ways to get your customers to fund growth, like Costco did.

Cash Acceleration Strategies (CASh)

To help teams brainstorm ways to improve their cash conversion cycles, we created a one-page tool called Cash Acceleration Strategies, or CASh. It breaks down the CCC into four main components:

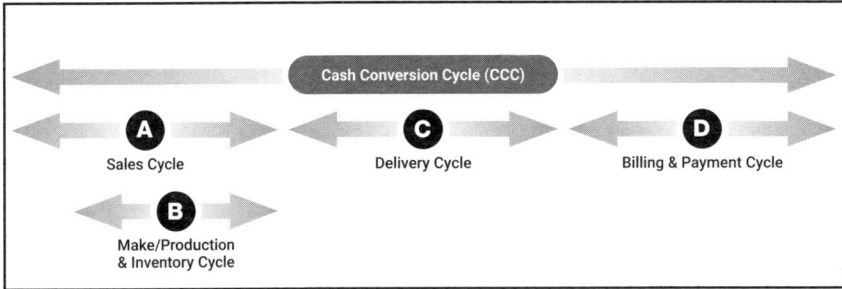

Most businesses will have some aspect of each of these cash cycle components. Even service firms have a form of inventory even if they have underutilized staff. What might differ is the sequence of these components, with some cycles overlapping others or occurring in a different order. For instance, if you've structured your business model to collect full payments in advance, like Dell, then the billing and payment cycle occurs after the selling cycle but before the production and delivery cycle. (In other words, Dell arranged to take ownership of inventory only after a computer was sold.)

We encourage management teams to set aside an hour or more each month to brainstorm ways to improve each of these cash cycle components. This is a powerful exercise to do with the broader middle-leadership team at a half- to full-day monthly leadership meeting. It will give everyone a better understanding of how cash flows through the business and how each function can contribute positively.

Some areas of opportunity:

- First, stop saying, "Well, this is just the way it is in our industry."
- Have your available cash reported DAILY, with a short explanation of why it changed in the last 24 hours, and chart it against accounts receivable (AR) and accounts payable (AP) weekly. You'll learn so much more about your business when you see how the cash is flowing on a daily basis. If you want to be paid sooner, ask. Small firms are finding that large companies (and governments!!)

will pay considerably faster or even prepay if you simply ask, ask, ask, ask, and ask some more.

- Give value back to customers who pay on time or in advance.
- Get your invoices out more quickly. Hire one more person in accounting to do nothing but make sure invoicing is timely and follow up on payments.
- Send friendly reminders five days *before* the deadline that payments are due. Many customers are disorganized and will appreciate the reminders, resulting in faster payment.
- If invoices are recurring, obtain recurring credit card authorization from your customers to automate on-time payments.
- Understand why your clients are paying late. They might be unhappy with your product or service. Or perhaps an invoice has recurring mistakes, or it is not structured to flow through the customer's automated invoicing system.
- Understand each customer's payment cycles, and time your billings to coincide.
- Pay many of your own expenses with a credit card so you can play the float. Get your own customers to pay by credit card, so they can pay you quickly even if their cash flow is slow.
- Help your customers improve their cash flow so they can pay you on time. Offer them leasing options, for instance.
- Shorten cycles for delivery of your product or service. All of you have some kind of "work in progress." The faster you complete projects, the faster you get paid.
- Offer a product or service so valuable that you have some leverage with your customers to get them to pay sooner.
- Remember, improving margins and profits improve cash.

NOTE: Have your CFO or controller give you a cash report every day, like mine does. The CFO should summarize the sources and amounts of cash that came in and out of the business during the last 24 hours, along with anticipated cash flow for the coming month. It keeps cash top-of-mind and allows you to react quickly—within days vs. months—if it's heading in the wrong direction. Observing the sources of cash flowing in and out on a daily basis also gives real insight into your business's financial model.

Almost all of these ideas fall into three general categories where you can make improvements:
1. Shorten cycle times.
2. Eliminate mistakes.
3. Change the business model.

To further stimulate your thinking, here are some ideas in each category that can help you improve cash flow.

Shorten Cycle Times

Increasing the pace of everything your company does (e.g., decreasing the time it takes to complete a full cycle from customer interest to completed transaction) helps your CCC. This is why we are fans of applying Toyota's Lean process to all aspects of the business. With its focus on eliminating wasted time, it's an ideal tool to improve processes, increase employee productivity, and accelerate cash flow.

Pay particular attention to the sales process. You may be expending enormous amounts of money and time on landing customers. Using negotiation techniques taught by Victoria Medvec (check out her powerful online "High Stakes Negotiation" course at *scalingup.com*), firms like Goldman Sachs have reduced sales cycles from months to weeks and from weeks to days. The quicker you can get a deal in the door, the quicker the cash starts flowing—and you thwart would-be competitors.

On the production side, back when Dell had factories, a production worker could assemble a computer in minutes, and the company held only a few days' worth of inventory. This rapid turn of inventory and the speed of manufacturing contributed hugely to the impressive CCC the company achieved.

Because many accounting departments are short-handed, there are often delays in getting invoices sent out and bills collected. Besides billing twice per month to improve cash flow, Catapult Systems collects faster than most firms. Notes Goodner, the former chairman: "Our collections person in the accounting department works hard to create a personal rapport with our clients' accounts payable teams. She is the most charming, disarming, nonthreatening, likable person you could possibly have. She starts calling the accounting departments of our clients five days before the check is due just to make sure everything is okay, and says that we are doing great on the project. She gives her number just in case anything comes up and says, 'I really look forward to getting that check from you next week.' " And if the check is late, the Catapult Systems' collections specialist places a call to the client the next day. That is another reason to bolster your accounting department resources.

Goodner credits this approach with his company's "unbelievably high" track record of getting paid on time—simply because, he says, "We ask for it."

Meanwhile, a firm in Australia sends inexpensive lottery tickets as thank-yous to its customers' accounts payable clerks when they pay invoices on time. When customers are faced with a stack of bills to pay, this company's invoices seem to magically make it to the top of the pile! And if this might be frowned upon (or deemed illegal) in your industry or locale, a holiday card showing appreciation to the people in accounts payable can achieve the same effect. The point is to have someone pay attention to the accounts payable people!

Also specify a due date (May 31, for example) on the invoice rather than include the standard "due in 30 days." Often, someone higher up in the client organization has to sign off on an invoice before it can be paid, with the 30-day clock starting when this signature is received. If there is a specific due date, even if the signature isn't obtained until the day before, the payables clerk will assume that the sign-off authorizes the payment to occur on the date specified, and will pay the bill immediately.

Examine all of the processes in the organization—sales, production, service delivery, billing, and collections—and find ways to speed up and move cash more quickly through the business.

Eliminate Mistakes

Nothing infuriates customers more than a mistake. It is the #1 reason they are slow to pay. And incomplete orders, invoicing errors, and missed deadlines are not only costly but also drag down the very processes you want to speed up, snarling cash flow.

Adam Sproule, third generation CEO of Salisbury Landscaping in Alberta, has the company's cash conversion cycle down to a fine art. The approach he has used has helped him optimize the CCC for the past 25+ years. Besides securing deposits up front (with the final payment due immediately upon a project's completion), Salisbury Landscaping has put operating practices in place to finish jobs quickly and in a far less disruptive way than clients usually see in its industry. This, in turn, has given Salisbury a reputation that makes collecting deposits and payments easier.

Tradespeople in landscaping or construction usually work on two to three jobs at the same time, often leaving customers wondering what's happening and why the projects aren't finished yet. "It's a real pet peeve of people we talk to," says Sproule. Instead, Salisbury's crews focus on one job at a time, getting in and out as quickly as possible. "We deal with live plants, so we want to finish quickly," Sproule says. "Not only is it a major disruption to our clients if we don't, but the longer we take, the more likely there will be problems."

As soon as the crew leaves, a member of Sproule's team walks around with the customer to make sure the job is absolutely perfect. "Even if there are just a couple deficiencies, we write them down," says Sproule, who notes that his staff refers to corrections of deficiencies as "adjustments," to avoid any negative perception.

"We then make an adjustment list. Because we're very efficient at what we do, the customer has no reason to doubt us. So a lot of times, they give us the full payment immediately after the walk-around even if there are a few things left to do," notes Sproule. And to close the loop of learning and avoid making the same mistakes on subsequent projects, Salisbury sends out the same crew that generated the deficiencies to handle the adjustments quickly.

PPR Talent Management Group (acquired by Medical Solutions in 2018) freed up a million dollars every month through improved accuracy in its invoicing. Serving the needs of a thousand clients—mostly hospitals, all with different policies and time-sheet protocols—caused considerable complexity in invoicing. As a result, clients delayed paying while PPR sorted out the errors on its invoices. To address this issue, the Florida company hired an additional person not only to build relationships with the payables departments but also to customize invoices to match each specific hospital's billing codes. As former CEO Dwight Cooper notes, "When we changed our process and got it right, the confidence level with our clients came up fast."

Then the latest recession came. As it dragged on into 2009, Cooper says, "We took our eye off the cash ball." It was time to change the entire business model—at least from a cash perspective.

Change the Business Model

For PPR, collections were not the problem; it was creating the right terms to begin with. To grow the business, PPR needed cash, so it asked customers to pay in advance. "We were pleasantly surprised when many of our customers just said yes," says Cooper.

There are many adjustments you can make to your business model that positively affect your CCC. The two with the biggest results are getting your customers to fund your business, much like Costco does via membership fees, or having suppliers do this, as Dell did through its inventory management.

For sources of cash other than loans or investors, read the *Fortune Small Business* article Verne wrote titled "Finding Money You Didn't Know You Had."

Improving Profitability

Benetton India also felt the crunch of the economic downturn in 2009, so it embarked on a major cost-saving initiative. Sanjeev Mohanty, CEO of Benetton India Private Ltd., got vendors to bid online for contracts using business-commerce software purchased from Ariba. "Initially, everyone was very skeptical, saying that we would lose quality," he says. Plus, some suppliers had been providing goods to Benetton India for more than a decade, and executives hesitated to disrupt what appeared to be working well.

Mohanty persisted, and the savings have been significant. For instance, Benetton India invited six different suppliers, including the incumbent, to bid on its contract for shopping bags. Suppliers can use Ariba not only to place their bids, but also to see what other companies are bidding. Normally, the whole bidding process can take several hours, but this round closed in 32 minutes, while the executive team watched in real time. Benetton previously paid 52 cents per shopping bag, and the final bid came in at 34 cents—a huge savings. Surprisingly, the incumbent supplier provided the final low bid, so in addition to benefiting from the savings, Benetton India maintained the

same-quality bag. Today, company employees must use Ariba to pro-
cure any goods or services with a value of more than $10,000. In one
recent year, Benetton India saved $1.2 million through this procure-
ment process.

Again, when you improve profitability, it improves cash—as long as
you're not funding management waste on the balance sheet, as we'll
discuss further in the next two chapters. And for retail companies like
MOM's Organic Market and Benetton India, which collect cash or credit card payments for every transaction, the only real internal financial
cash lever is on the P&L side of the business.

During the recent financial crisis, fearing credit lines might dry up,
MOM's CEO Scott Nash and his team stayed laser-focused on improving profitability (emphasizing pricing, purchasing, etc.). Today, with
four times industry average profitability, the metro Washington-based
chain has driven up its free operating cash flow to fund its continued
expansion. At Catapult Systems, Goodner found cost savings by sitting
down with an accounts payable employee every six months to scrutinize what the company is paying for goods and services. Understanding
the expenses, one-time charges, and recurring charges leads to savings
opportunities that add up. "There's probably tens of thousands of dollars a year I can cut, and the company doesn't feel the difference,"
Goodner says. For example, when he realized that the company was
paying $600 per month for bottled-water service at one office, he decid
ed to purchase a commercial filtration system instead, for one-tenth of
the cost. "Recurring charges are the ones that really kill you," says
Goodner. "Anything that's a recurring charge forever, I still personally
approve before it gets accepted."

Completing Your
Cash Acceleration Strategies (CASh) Tool

1. Read the *Harvard Business Review* article by Neil C. Churchill and
   John W. Mullins titled "How Fast Can Your Company Afford to
   Grow?"
2. Calculate your existing CCC in days.
3. Calculate the amount of cash required to fund each additional
   day of CCC.

4. Brainstorm ways to improve your CCC and the 7 financial levers highlighted in the last chapter of this "Cash" section using the one-page CASh tool. Be sure to explore ways in all three general categories—shortening cycle times, eliminating mistakes, and changing the business model—for each segment of the CCC.
5. Choose one cash-improvement initiative every 90 days as one of your quarterly priorities (Rocks).

Imagine you improve your CCC by 30 days (and you run a $30 million business). You now have $2.5 million extra in your bank account, and you can:
1. Pay down your operating credit line.
2. Distribute a dividend to shareholders.
3. Invest in a new project that will support your growth plans.
4. Sit on it until you find the perfect opportunity.
5. Keep it as insurance for when times get rough.

The best part about improving your CCC is that it usually results in your business pulsing faster, which is better for the customer. It will also improve the business savvy of your managers as they become more aware of the impact of their decisions on cash flow. And with more cash in the bank, everyone will sleep better as you scale up the business. This is one routine that will really set you free and give you sticking power in the market.

The key to improving cash flow and profitability is investing more in the accounting side of the business. It's hard to make intelligent decisions without data.

Accounting: Underappreciated

If the #1 weakness of growth firms is marketing, the #2 problem is accounting. Accounting is often underappreciated. It is seen as a necessary evil to keep the tax collectors at bay; invoice, collect, and pay bills; and provide monthly accounting statements—which often receive at most a cursory glance at the bottom line of the P&L.

Accounting is often underfunded as a result. Most entrepreneurs, if they have an extra dollar of profit to spend, invest it in either making or selling stuff. Those are good uses of the money. However, we've seen profits and cash double within a year when businesspeople also devote just a little more attention and resources to accounting (remember,

John D. Rockefeller was an accountant by training). Hiring just one additional person to either support the CFO or carry some of this executive's workload enables him or her to provide the following:
1. Better cash and cash-flow management
2. Waterfall graphs, which we will explain shortly, to share more granular accounting data for better decision-making
3. Trend analysis and early-warning systems to support better prediction
4. Two sets of books—for the right reasons!

Waterfall Graphs

A key accounting activity is to slice and dice a company's financial data as granularly as possible. This lets the leadership team view the gross margin, profit, and cash flow by categories, such as individual customer, location, product line, salesperson, etc. Accountants do this by creating a series of waterfall graphs (see the diagram below).

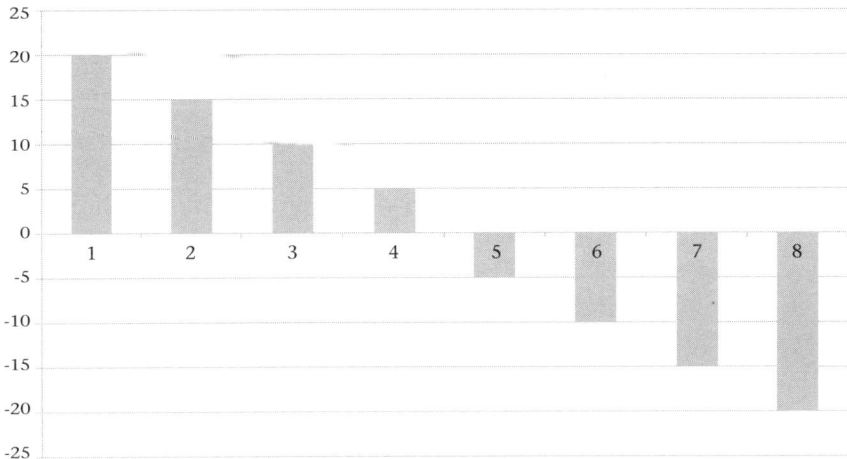

NOTE: The vertical axis might measure gross margin or profit percentage, while the horizontal axis might enumerate specific customers, locations, salespeople, product lines, or SKUs.

The leadership team soon discovers from these waterfall graphs that the company is making a bunch of money from a limited part of the business and losing some or a lot in other parts, resulting in a gross margin or profitability that is mediocre. It's the less profitable parts of the business that tend to suck up most of management's time and attention. It was a series of waterfall graphs that Dell CFO Tom Meredith presented to Michael Dell and the leadership team to convince them to change their business model and move out of 40% of the product lines and distribution channels they were in.

Turnaround specialists like Greg Brenneman, the Houston-based chairman of private equity firm TurnWorks Inc., also rely on this kind of data to eliminate consistently unprofitable routes, as he did at Continental Airlines, and menu items, as he did at the Quiznos restaurant chain.

So why do we continue to hold on to these losers? "For strategic reasons" is the excuse! Yet what is strategic about losing lots of money over a long period of time? Apple could have easily argued that selling its money-losing handheld computers was a strategic move, but Steve Jobs eliminated the product line when he came back to run the firm a second time. Any loss leaders you might need—and these should be kept to a minimum—should be treated as a marketing expense in your accounting. For more insight into this common strategic mistake, read Brenneman's *Harvard Business Review* case study on the turnaround of Continental Airlines.

Trend Analysis

A fundamental responsibility of leaders is prediction, and they need both frequent quantitative data and qualitative feedback from the market to make the right calls. As we've mentioned, any data more than a week old is history and is not useful for making the fast decisions necessitated by our highly connected global economy.

The accounting function is critical in this regard. It should provide the kinds of reports and graphs that help the leadership team see into the near future. For example, we helped the CFO of a distributor of electrical supplies to set up a series of weekly bar charts (rather than eye-straining Excel spreadsheets) that monitored major customers' purchases of various product lines. Sales to these accounts constituted 80% of the firm's revenue.

After a few months, the company could see that one of the customers was slowly reducing its relative order size. That was an early warning that something was amiss and alerted the account manager to follow up more quickly than normal. The company was also quicker to notice and act on other trends, like the change in popularity of certain product lines, now that leaders were seeing this visual data weekly, rather than monthly or quarterly.

Mapping Software

Where are all the maps with pushpins you used to see populating sales and marketing offices—and the offices of CEOs? We wish companies used them more. Seeing data mapped out this way helps you visualize patterns you wouldn't otherwise discern. For instance, we mapped a database of scaleups against cities where we have coaching partners and could immediately see where we had gaps in our coverage.

Barrett Ersek used a series of maps and Microsoft's powerful MapPoint software (replaced by Bing Maps in 2015) to see patterns in where he was making sales (based on close ratios) and getting callbacks within his lawn care business.

See how many Excel spreadsheets you can replace using mapping software, and encourage your accounting team to create more maps.

Two Sets of Books

One set of accounting books is needed to satisfy the rules of the Financial Accounting Standards Board (FASB) and the tax authorities. However, rarely should you make business decisions based solely on these regulations. For instance, computer hardware and software can be amortized over several years for tax purposes. However, Michael Dell wanted business units to implement only solutions that had a quick payoff. So, for internal purposes, Dell treated all technology costs as an expense against a division's P&L within 12 months.

For more on this topic, we encourage all CFOs to read Thomas A. Stewart's classic book *Intellectual Capital: The New Wealth of Organizations*. Pay particular attention to the extensive appendix, where he suggests specific accounting rules that better align with an information-based economy than with a manufacturing-type economy, which generated many of the FASB rules we follow today. For example, whereas you can amortize software over several years, you must expense employee training and development in the quarter in which it's provided. Stewart argues strongly that if any expense could legitimately be amortized over a longer period of time, it is education.

The ideas your team learns today will continue to have an impact for many years.

The key is to decide on the practices and rules by which you want the company to run, and have accounting align your internal books in support. Use Stewart's book as your guide to grow a 21st-century-focused organization.

Gross Margin Dollars

Revenue is vanity (and the weakest number) when it comes to your P&L. Focus instead on a redefined version of gross margin to be revenue minus all NONLABOR direct costs. This definition of gross margin gives you the true economic top line of the business.

Understanding this is especially important for businesses that utilize subcontractors, have high materials costs, or operate as distributors with low margins. There is no way that a $4 million distributor that gets a 10 percent commission on all its sales or a custom home builder with high costs for materials and subcontractors compares to a $4 million service firm. In essence, nonlabor direct costs, which are paid out of revenue, are simply pass-throughs. You definitely want to get them at the best price, but you usually cannot move the price enough to make up for any profit deficiency in your business model. The same holds true at employment agencies and professional employee organizations, where revenue is the total payroll that passes through the organization. The net dollars they have to operate their businesses are a fraction of this amount.

In most service-companies, gross margin dollars becomes the new top-line focus, instead of revenue. This guides the business to seek opportunities that result in the highest gross margin per labor dollar. This is a key step in going from breakeven to 10 percent profitability and beyond.

Instead of obsessing about revenue, shift the internal discussions to generating gross margin, the real top line of the business. (Talk about revenue with outsiders if you want.) And note: The focus is more on gross margin dollars than gross margin as a percentage.

4X Industry Average GM$/Employee

Andy Bailey took this advice to heart at his firm NationLink Wireless, a chain of telecommunication retail stores. When he started implementing Scaling Up his gross margin dollars per employee was $75,000. By focusing each quarter on ways to improve this KPI, seven years later he drove that number to $275,000 gross margin dollars per employee, 4x industry average. This allowed him to exit for an outsized valuation.

Please start tracking this critical KPI, which has a tendency to drop as the company scales (because we "throw people at the problems").

The Power of Gross Margin

Gross margin doesn't get enough respect. It's bad enough that it's stuck in the middle of the P&L and often gets glossed over. It's actually THE most powerful indicator of an effective sales team, a differentiated strategy, and real growth. As a company scales up, the market demands better pricing (e.g., your largest customers now ask for discounts). When this is combined with the complexities and increasing costs that come with being a larger company, we often see gross margins shrink by 3% to 4%—from, say, 55.4% to 51.8%. At the $10 million or $100 million level, such a dip results in $300,000 to $3 million becoming unavailable to fund infrastructure, pay a key executive, or fuel profitability.

There are two options to improve your gross margins. The first is to refine your strategy to maintain enough differentiation and uniqueness in your offering that you can hold your line on pricing (see "The 7 Strata of Strategy" chapter). This requires both salespeople who can sell this differentiation and a marketing function that keeps them armed and focused on the right customers. In these cases, you can actually see gross margins increase a few percentage points with growth. This is why hyperspecialization is powerful.

Of course, there are some markets that are just brutal—especially for lower-margin products and services. In these cases, if you get too focused on the gross margin percentage, you may miss an opportunity to grow, and your only option is to simply drive up overall gross margin dollars. That last gross margin dollar shouldn't cost you as much as the first one, so bring in as much cash as you can, factoring in how you might have to ramp up fixed costs.

If the market tells you the price that customers are willing to pay, you have to make your costs fit and still turn a profit. This is called a cost-led pricing strategy.

WARNING: Since gross margin dollars more accurately measure sales performance, you should never base sales compensation on revenue unless your cost of goods sold does not vary from sale to sale. You will be paying commissions on revenue while allowing your salespeople to set the price!

NOTE: If you enjoyed this book, read Verne Harnish's newest title *Scaling Up: How a Few Companies Make It...and Why the Rest Don't (Rockefeller Habits 2.0)*

Concluding Thoughts

You can get by with decent People, decent Strategy, decent Execution, but not a day without Cash.

My dad ran out of cash, and it cost him his very successful business – and his health. I ran out of cash immediately following 9/11 and thought I might face the same until I took some of our own advice.

What I've shared comes from over four decades of helping leaders scale easier with less drama. Please let us know how we can be of service to you and your team through coaching, training, and a robust tech platform.

Please visit *www.scalingup.com* for a bunch of free resources including our Growth Tools in multiple languages and a complimentary one-hour "Scaling Up" mini-course you can share with your team—15 minutes each for People, Strategy, Execution, and Cash.

And when you're ready for a more comprehensive set of tools/tech- niques for scaling, please check out our book *Scaling Up: How a Few Companies Make It...and Why the Rest Don't.*

Keep Scaling!

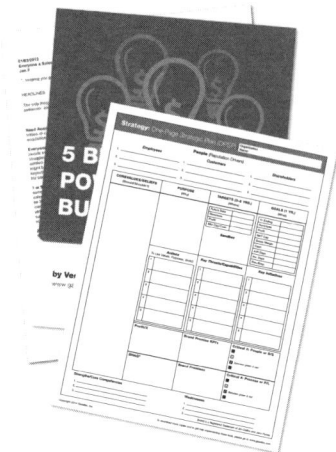